The Guide to Earned Media

The Guide to Earned Media

How to Use PR Strategies to
Enhance Your Brand

Annie Pace Scranton

KoganPage

First published in Great Britain and the United States in 2023 by Kogan Page Limited

2nd Floor, 45 Gee Street	8 W 38th Street, Suite 902	4737/23 Ansari Road
London	New York, NY 10018	Daryaganj
EC1V 3RS	USA	New Delhi 110002
United Kingdom		India
www.koganpage.com		

© Annie Pace Scranton, 2023

The right of Annie Pace Scranton to be identified as the author of this work has been asserted by her in accordance with the Copyright, Designs and Patents Act 1988.

ISBNs

Hardback	9781398611078
Paperback	9781398611054
Ebook	9781398611061

British Library Cataloguing-in-Publication Data
A CIP record for this book is available from the British Library.

Library of Congress Control Number
2023940509

Typeset by Hong Kong FIVE Workshop, Hong Kong
Print production managed by Jellyfish
Printed and bound by CPI Group (UK) Ltd, Croydon CR0 4YY

Kogan Page books are printed on paper from sustainable forests.

To those of us who work in the public relations industry.

*A career in PR is exciting and highly-rewarding,
but at times it can be a rollercoaster, filled with ups and
downs. I hope this book will help you to maximize the highs
and coast through the lows a bit easier.*

CONTENTS

I

FOREWORD

by Mary Corcoran, President, North America, BCW

In today's fast-paced and ever-changing press, the importance of earned media cannot be overstated. With the rise of social media and digital advertising, many organizations and brands have shifted their focus away from traditional PR methods, such as pitching stories to journalists and building relationships with media outlets. However, the value of authentic and honest communication has only grown as the world becomes increasingly inundated with disinformation.

This is where Annie Pace Scranton comes in. As a true master of the lost art of earned media, she possesses a rare level of expertise and nuance in today's PR industry. What truly sets Annie apart is her commitment to excellence. She has taken the skills she learned as a booker and applied them to the world of PR, becoming a master of earned media and communication. She understands that earned media is not just about securing coverage; it's about telling a story that resonates with a target audience and building trust with stakeholders.

This book is a valuable resource for anyone who wants to learn how to tell their story effectively. Whether you are an entrepreneur looking to build your brand, a nonprofit trying to raise awareness of your cause, or an individual looking to connect with others on a deeper level, this book is for you. Annie breaks down the art of storytelling into simple, easy-to-understand steps that anyone can follow. In addition, she provides practical advice and real-world examples that will help you craft a story that is both compelling and authentic.

Annie's book is not just a guide to storytelling; it is a manifesto for a better world. It is a call to action for all of us to embrace the power of our own stories, to share them with others, and to listen to the stories of those around us. It is a reminder that we are all connected, that our stories are intertwined and that we can build a better future by sharing them.

The importance of effective PR and earned media cannot be over-stated. It is crucial that businesses, organizations, and individuals understand how to communicate in a way that is truthful and authentic. And that is exactly what Annie's book provides. It is a roadmap for success grounded in transparency and credibility. I know it will be an invaluable resource for anyone looking to succeed in PR and communications.

Introduction

Bill Gates is believed to have said: "If I was down to my last dollar, I'd spend it on public relations."

The power of public relations is real. I've done my best throughout this book to give examples from my 20-plus years of working in PR and the media to show rather than tell real instances of how PR has truly made an impact for our clients. As you'll read, and hopefully absorb, PR can mean a lot of different things to a lot of different people. Earned media is only one slice of the greater field that is PR— and it's truly an important one.

Writing a book has always been a bucket-list item for me, as I think it is for a lot of people. Having the chance to write about the work I do day-in and day-out has been a joy and a privilege. I've noticed a keen interest for years, since the very beginning of my career, from so many folks who are simply fascinated by what I do. To them, the media is sexy… it's intriguing. People are always wondering, "How did that person get on TV? How could I get on TV?" These are the beginnings of many conversations I have with prospective clients.

So writing a book on the topic makes sense, given people's obsession with the media. However, what I've tried to outline in this book is a step-by-step guide for readers who haven't had the opportunity yet to either study public relations or work in the industry. PR is one of those fields where you can learn a lot from reading on your own, surfing the web or listening to relevant podcasts. There are advanced degrees in PR (I received one at NYU—and now teach in their PR Master's program!)… but the requirements are not as vigorous as, say, studying medicine or the law. For this reason, a lot of people think they can "do" PR… and maybe they can. But without proper training and guidance, it will be nearly impossible to maintain the ever-constant wheel that is PR and earned media.

I hope that's where this book comes in handy. PR is an industry that many often "fall into." Some wind up slowly taking on communications efforts, without it even being part of their current job description. Some are actually doing the full job of a comms manager or director—without having it in their current job description. Since PR is a field that so many start working in without receiving relevant formal training or education, hopefully this book will serve as a supplement to help fill in some of those learning gaps, if not serve as a roadmap for how to secure earned media.

So... what is PR, anyway? That's what we'll dive into in the very first chapter of this book, along with defining "earned media," a subset of PR. Media relations is the practice of securing earned media placements (placements are interviews, stories, segments, etc.). Public relations encompasses many subset, specialty areas but for the context of this book the definition we'll use of PR is that it is the practice of partnering with and understanding your client and then helping them to reach their goals, via excellent earned media placements.

Branding is another focus in Chapter 1. Branding is PR's counterpart. It's impossible to have a successful PR campaign if you don't have the branding nailed down for your client. Some of you reading this may not even know how to define branding, let alone how to think about it for your clients. That's okay. We're going to give you a working definition and then lay out different scenarios, with roadmaps, on how you can successfully lead a branding initiative or campaign for your clients.

Chapter 2 lays out the three main spheres of influence within the practice of media relations: print, digital and broadcast. When writing this book, I have assumed that the reader has little, if any, background in the media. So this chapter goes into a ton of detail on the history of each sphere—and the transformations that have occurred over the years. Print, digital, and broadcast media have undergone sweeping changes in the past few decades and continue to evolve and change in real time. Many often will question whether these traditional media outlets will still be relevant in our society in forthcoming years, asking if social media and other new media forums will instead hold more value for brands over traditional media outlets. I am a huge proponent of traditional media, as you'll realize as you read on, and I hope I've made a strong case for them.

Before you can accurately begin any earned media work for your company or client, you need to understand the origin story of that company or client. This is what Chapter 3 focuses on. It may sound simple, but I've seen time and time again over the years that many faithful long-term employees just don't know how the company they work for got its start. As you'll see later on in Chapter 6, without knowing the origin story, you'll be unable to do a whole slice of work in the thought leadership category for your client. I outline strategies and advice for how to get to the heart of the origin story for your client or company in a way that will be efficient and streamlined. This will require getting face time with the founder and/or C-suite executives, which I realize may not be easy. I offer up some tactics around how to navigate this potentially challenging situation.

Next up in Chapter 4 we dive into setting goals. If you have no goals in life things will just happen to you, instead of you having agency over what you want your life to be. This is true, I believe, in all areas of our lives, but certainly in your career and job. I outline various exercises on how to set goals—both for yourself professionally, and in terms of tactical goals you want to meet in the media relations arena. I've been fortunate in my career where my day-to-day goals always, in some way, sync up with my bigger picture career goals. I think that's the sign of someone who is in an industry that is well suited to them. I also believe that the best publicists do their best work because they are immersed in the industry. If you *love* what you do, you're going to be more successful. PR can be a grind. It can be grueling and frustrating on many different levels. But it can also be wildly rewarding. I believe setting goals will lead to the rewarding aspects quicker. Once you start "winning" there's a good chance you may get hooked on PR!

Now that you know the origin story of your client and you've set your goals and you have a good understanding of PR, branding, and the media, it's time to practice. Yes—in Chapter 5, I actually lay out techniques to first practice your brand's elevator pitch, before you start pitching the media. It's amazing to me how many times a CEO, let alone their publicist, just cannot describe the essence of their company—what they do and what return on investment (ROI) they offer to their own customers or clients—in less than 60 seconds. Generally speaking, I ask every single prospective client to do this for me. Many cannot—and often then say, "Wow. I guess I should work on that."

Um, yes. They have to—and you have to, if you're going to be successful at pitching earned media. An elevator pitch is essentially how you "sell" your company or your client, in 30–60 seconds—as if you were stuck in the elevator with your dream journalist—this is your chance to make it or break it! I go through, in much more detail, the various elements of an elevator pitch, exercises to get the creative juices flowing and then granular tips for how to create your own. These tactics can be applied for your clients—but also for yourself. Remember, so much of PR is actually selling yourself... we'll get into that later on in the book, but I hope this chapter will inspire you to come up with your own elevator pitch, as a first step towards feeling comfortable sharing with others who you are, what you're great at, and why they need to know about you!

Chapter 6 is all about thought leadership—a buzzy phrase that is used constantly in PR. I go through the definition of thought leadership, and the various ways you can start thinking about implementing it throughout your earned media relations work. Thought leadership, often used interchangeably with subject matter expertise, is aligning the CEO or founder as an industry leader—someone who has the foresight to spot trends and have an opinion on industry news that will be relevant and helpful, if shared publicly.

Publicists can help with thought leadership internally, via owned media to start. This means that publicists can work with their client's CEO or founder on blog posts, LinkedIn messaging or via any of your company's own marketing tools, such as a podcast or newsletter. I go through the steps needed to begin this work. Once you're in a groove on the owned media side it's a natural transition to start pitching your client in a thought leadership style to the media. We will dive into op-eds and contributor articles as one main tactic and then how to position your client to reporters covering relevant industries in which you could become a resource for expert quotes and/or opinions.

The next two chapters take a very deep dive into the art of pitching, something I, and the other publicists at my agency, do every single day. Chapter 7 starts off with pitching print and digital media. I try to offer up as many real examples as possible of how to connect with reporters in a way that's going to yield a response. The first aspect we cover is the research—meaning, making sure, prior to pitching, you've researched the reporter and the outlet so that you can write the most informed pitch possible. Pitching is personal, and having a personal touch with the way in which you reach out to a reporter is so important. Reporters and producers are people, too... you don't want to send pitches that are robotic or read like a term paper. In this chapter we spend a lot of time figuring out how to get right to the point you're trying to make—all while remembering, would this be of interest to the reporter, and if they wrote the story you pitched what would the reader at home gain from the piece? Remembering to think about the ROI in everything you do is key.

Chapter 8 is all about pitching to TV producers, which is similar, of course, to pitching to print and digital reporters, but with some nuances for sure. TV producers are working, usually, under even shorter and more frequent deadlines than print or digital reporters. Many actually produce a brand-new show each and every day, meaning that they have a lot of air time to continually fill. The relationship between a publicist and the media is symbiotic—we need them and they need us. But if we don't understand the basics of their job, and the basics of what kinds of segments they produce, we are seen as a detriment to their job—someone who wastes their time and can be seen as annoying.

This is why—again—the research element is so critically important. I offer up steps to take to actually get to know the network and the show you are pitching. It's not rocket science—actually just watching the show you're pitching will, most of the time, give you a good sense of the focus of the program. But we also dive into how you can get to know the producers and the anchors of these shows, even if it's from afar—social media being the number one resource publicists have in their corner. This chapter will also bring home the point on how important it is to develop actual, real relationships with producers, and offers some tips on how to begin to form those relationships.

Finally, in Chapter 9 we discuss speaking engagements. Live speaking opportunities are a frequent request from clients who are interested in earned media opportunities. Often the most challenging part of working on securing speaking engagements is, once again, the research. There are so many potential opportunities in the United States and internationally that a good portion of your time will likely be spent on researching these various conferences and events. I offer up strategies for how to narrow in on the type of audiences your client wants to be in front of and then how to source live speaking opportunities for those audiences. The process of applying as a speaker is similar to earned media pitching, but with some slight differences, which we'll discuss.

I hope you enjoy reading this book and will learn enough about PR and earned media to feel as though you are set up for success as you embark on this journey.

PR and Successful Branding

How do you *do* PR? A common refrain is that PR is learned on the job. But what if you're the lone person in your organization's comms department? It's not a widely-offered major or graduate program. I've heard countless professionals say that they were suddenly "gifted" the "opportunity" to run point on PR because they got one placement or created a social media post that performed well. While that is a nod to their creativity and hard work ethic, it often can feel a little lonely working in PR for a corporation, especially if there is no one to help you work through the inevitable challenges we all face. Hopefully this book will serve as that guidepost for you, as you aim to successfully navigate the highs, and lows, of PR.

So, What Exactly Is PR?

The value of PR is often extremely challenging to quantify. But the qualitative results, when executed correctly, can make all the difference in the world. According to the Public Relations Society of America, the leading US-based organization dedicated to the profession, "Public relations is a strategic communication process that builds mutually beneficial relationships between organizations and their publics."[1] Essentially: PR is what gets you noticed. You can have the greatest company, product or brand in the world, but if no one knows about it, what good does it do?

Let's discuss briefly what PR is not. The chances are high that someone you work with or report to—perhaps the CEO, a founder, or an investor—doesn't understand the differences between marketing and PR. PR is *not* marketing, advertising, social media, digital, or content creation.

According to the Oxford Learner's Dictionaries, marketing is the action or business of promoting and selling products or services, including market research and advertising.[2] Oftentimes, corporations will have a marketing budget and PR is likely a component of that budget. Marketing encompasses any and all ways in which a business promotes itself, thus including, potentially, public relations, advertising, SEO, social media, and many other promotional avenues. Marketing, in a singular sense, tends to mean how a company reaches out *directly* to its customer or potential customer base.

Great marketing involves persistence and research. Persistence requires a lot of outreach, and research ensures that you are getting as many details as possible about a customer's interests and prospective interests.

Have you ever purchased a pair of shoes from a new brand you love and then all of a sudden you're getting weekly emails from said brand, letting you know about a new sale or a new product offering? Marketing. Have you then opened up Instagram and scratched your head wondering, "Well, that's strange… There's an ad for that same shoe brand!" That falls within marketing. The brand is targeting *you* very specifically, based on research of your buying habits.

Advertising is another form of marketing. This form is transactional, meaning that a company pays money to a media outlet to promote their business, brand or product. Glossy magazines have print ads. Commercials are also a form of advertising. Pop-ups before you watch a new YouTube video are ads. Advertising takes a large budget—it is "paid," after all, and it works when it seeps into your subconscious without you even realizing it.

Case in point: I was (and still am) completely obsessed with those Lincoln commercials that feature Matthew McConaughey. I love his voice. I love the way they were shot. I love how I feel when I watch those ads. As a viewer, I was a bit thrown when I first watched one of these, and the ad seemed to actually make me want to buy a Lincoln…

I know better than to fall for advertising, because I know so much about what goes into it. Ultimately, though, these commercials did push me to suggest that we test a Lincoln when we were eventually on the market for a car. (That was years ago, and we are happy Lincoln car owners to this day.)

Public relations is different from marketing and advertising—in fact, it's quite different.

According to the Oxford Reference dictionary: Public relations is the professional maintenance of a favorable public image by a company or other organization or a famous person.[3] Good PR can shape a company's image. It can make or break a CEO, a start-up, or a political candidate. At some point, any successful business will invest in PR. It's inevitable. But to what end? And how do you do it successfully?

This book is going to focus on just this by walking you through the principles of *earned media*. Simply put, "earned media" consists of any material written, recorded, or broadcast about your company that you did not pay for and that you did not create yourself.

Paid media is advertising. In other words, a company is paying a hefty sum to circulate an ad or a commercial. *Owned media* means just that: you own it yourself. It's great to create content on your own (and we'll get into this later on in the book) for your website and your social media channels. But nothing—nothing—within the greater context of marketing has the ability to bring real value the way that earned media can.

So how do you go about securing earned media for your business?

Securing earned media relies a lot on your ability to tell the story of the company you're a part of. But how do you go about doing this? This book will break down this very thing for you—how to understand the origin story of the founder and the business, to really deeply feel as though you can communicate the brand's ethos in a palatable way, all of which is leading up to the endgame: that press placement that will help in paving the way towards more brand awareness.

An important thing to understand about PR and securing earned media is that it's all speculative. Really. No publicist—I don't care how experienced they are—has a smoking gun that will *guarantee* that they can generate earned media for their clients. They can point to their incredible case studies and track records and recent press placements. They can point to years of successfully being in business. They can point towards the many media contacts they have and know and work with routinely. But, it's still not something that can be guaranteed.

The other thing that's very important to know about PR is that it does not directly lead to increased sales. If your boss comes to you and says, "I really want you to focus on PR so we can increase our sales," you need to do whatever it takes to quickly educate her or him about the nuances of PR vs. sales or advertising. Have I seen clients dramatically increase their company's bottom line after a string of amazing earned media placements? Absolutely. Have I also gotten clients incredible hits which garnered very little in terms of traction? Unfortunately, yes.

A quick real-life example. I had a client several years ago who was an author based in Minneapolis. She hired us to help promote her first published book, on the importance of sleep, which weaved in some of her own personal narrative. She was telegenic, smart, and up for anything. We had a great run promoting the book, but the biggest moment of the campaign—and still, to this day, one of the biggest, best, and most fun bookings I've ever had—was when she was asked to appear as a guest on the TV show *Live! With Kelly and Michael*.

As a publicist, this is a dream booking come true. A beloved national network talk show in the United States, with a high viewership and great track record for fun segments. The producers definitely leaned into that fun when we started shaping this segment. They wanted to actually have my client do the segment *in her pajamas*, along with Kelly and Michael—also in their pajamas—with a king-sized bed as a prop on set.

The segment was fantastic—it was about six minutes (long for TV!). They started out by standing at the foot of the bed, asking the author questions about the book. Then they *all got into bed together* and she gave them sleep masks to put on, turned on the noise machine, talked about the importance of high-quality sheets, and they all pretended to take a snooze. At the beginning and end of the segment they flashed her book cover on screen and stated the title.

It was exciting—we were buzzing afterwards and couldn't wait to see the results. Would her website crash? Would her book sell thousands of copies on Amazon? It was all so exciting!

But we had to rush so she could get to a quiet place for her next interview—a local radio show from her hometown of Minneapolis. It was a drive time show, so a great slot... but an appearance that in no way had the same reach as *Live!*

My client called me the next day with some really surprising news to share. She relayed that, as a result of the TV appearance, she had received countless calls, texts, and messages on social media. Her old third grade teacher, a friend she'd lost touch with, her parents' neighbors—you name it, they all reached out because they had either seen the segment or heard about it. But when she tracked the sales from the time of day that she had been on TV and any sales linked to *Live's* online promotion of the book, the numbers were not that impressive. In fact, she hadn't really seen a significant increase at all after doing the show.

But what was *most* shocking was the fact that the local drive time radio show with the guy in Minneapolis had resulted in a couple hundred book sales!

We couldn't believe it. This was the first real eye-opening experience I had with earned media. I would have bet any amount of money that the national TV hit would have led to more book sales. But when I started really analyzing the situation and thinking about it, it (sort of) started to make sense. Let's think about the viewers of *Live!* It's on from 9–10 a.m. Most of the viewers are rushing around to get out the door, cleaning up after their kids have just left the house, or are just starting their day. They are *passive* viewers, likely with the TV just on in the background. They may have caught part of the segment with them in bed, gave a chuckle, and moved on. Likely, they were not paying close attention to who the expert guest was in the segment.

Now, the drive time radio show—that's a captive audience. If you're listening, you're likely driving. And if you're driving, you're just driving. You're not talking, you're not texting (hopefully), and you're sort of locked into the show at hand. I guarantee you those couple hundred listeners truly enjoyed the segment, walked away with some news they could use, and when they parked at their office took out their smartphones, and ordered my client's book.

I've also seen the exact opposite work with another former client, who is a meteorologist at a major cable news network. He created and developed a smart umbrella that he took to market with our help. He was able to book himself on the very morning show where he provided the weather to the audience. The channel really did him a solid and, again, provided quite a long segment for him to explain and showcase how the umbrella worked, with a live demo including a wind machine to illustrate the umbrella's strength in a rainstorm.

I was standing off-stage with a member of his team. He had his computer open to the back end of the umbrella's website, and we could see the sales in real time. It was unbelievable. In a six-minute segment they sold tens of thousands of dollars' worth of products, and the sales continued in the days that followed as he continued to promote on social media using the link he publicized on the show.

The bottom line is: PR does not equal sales. It can; it *certainly* can. But it's not a guarantee.

Branding 101

Chances are you, the reader, may not have a clear understanding of what the term "branding" means. Later in this chapter, you'll hear first-hand from someone who's made an entire career out of helping people, products, and brands themselves understand, discover, and then project their branding to the world. But, for now, here is how most publicists would describe branding.

Branding is how you describe your client. It's what you stand for. It's your belief system. It's the image you put forth and, traditionally, this is one your potential clients aspire to.

The beautiful thing about branding is that literally every single one of us can develop our own personal brand, should we choose to. Branding doesn't need to be exclusively reserved for large companies or well-known products. At some point, every single person, product, or company *needs* to codify their branding if they want to continue to be successful, meaning that, at some point, you may need to develop language bigger than yourself in order to continue to reach your target audience.

Let's start with personal branding, something that is deeply important to me as a female business owner and champion of women in business. What does being a woman have to do with personal branding? Chances are, at least half of you reading this book are female. The chances are much higher that you work with or report to a female. But, unfortunately, women currently only earn 84 percent to their male counterparts, despite our contribution to the workforce (and home lives).[4] A personal brand is a step that women can take to help ensure their financial future via a flourishing career.

How, you ask? How can a personal brand help a woman—or any human, for that matter—make more money or have a successful career? The answer is quite simple. For any of us to be successful in this world, you *have* to stand out. Whether you work for a large corporation, a small business, or are an entrepreneur, without knowing what makes you and your skillset unique, you can, and likely will, be overlooked.

Furthermore, today there's more competition than ever before. On average, every one corporate job opening attracts 250 resumes and only about five people get called for an interview.[5] And if you're a woman the facts are even more dismal. Women are a whopping 13 percent less likely to get promoted according to a recent survey by McKinsey.[6]

Think about it—how many others do you know in your industry with a similar skillset? How many other aspiring PR professionals do you know? How many others have tried their hand at working in communications in some capacity? There are a *lot* of us out there, and PR isn't an industry for the faint of heart. You have to have a thick skin, get used to the media rejecting you and, sometimes, work with unreasonable bosses. However, the upside can be so incredibly rewarding that I want to make sure you're set up to succeed as much as possible.

Figuring Out Your Personal Brand

So, let's back up. What is a personal brand? Simply put, your own personal brand is your calling card. Without a clear-cut personal brand, your reputation is in jeopardy. We live in a critical time where one's reputation can be threatened by one rogue tweet. A personal brand can *protect* you from such vulnerabilities, mainly because, once you have solidified your own brand, you will begin to live it and become an embodiment of it. And then if someone tries to threaten it, you will be able to call upon numerous examples supporting your impeccable character.

How do you figure out your own personal brand? The first step, and one I will revert back to time and time again in this book, is to work out your goals. What are they? I'm not talking just professionally, but personally too. Let's face it, we live in a world now where very few of us have a complete and total separation between our work and home lives. So you have to make sure your job and career are working for you, not just that you're working for them.

Here are some first, general issues to think about and undertake when determining a personal brand:

1 Always be honest. Don't pretend to be someone you're not—that's when you get into trouble.
2 Set realistic expectations.
3 Be consistent across all areas, whether that's in meetings, on social media, or over email.
4 Know your key strengths and play to them.

Brand yourself as the best version of yourself that you want to be. By putting that version of yourself forward, even when you're not quite confident you're there yet, you can trick yourself into meeting this demand. Psychologists call this cognitive dissonance.

Highlight your strengths in everything you do. Think of your résumé as *showing* what you do, and your personal brand as showing *how* you do it.

Here are some fun examples of personal brands to get your wheels turning:

- Are you a shark? Fearless and unafraid to take what's yours? Kill or be killed mentality?
- Are you a multitasker? Known for being able to take on multiple assignments at once and doing them all expertly?
- Are you an organizer? Pass the spreadsheet please!
- Are you a "get it done" type? Give me an assignment and it'll be done in an hour.

Maintaining Your Personal Brand

Now that you have given some thought to your personal brand, here are some simple steps to take to be sure you are the living embodiment of it:

- Make it a part of your routine. Practice it every day.
- Remember, you only have one shot at a first impression.
- Create a personal website. Treat it as your personal branding resume.
- Routinely update all of your social media handles with content and POV that is in line with your personal brand.

Remember, even if you're reading this and thinking to yourself "No one cares about me, or what I do. I don't have a reputation to protect." You're wrong. If you have a Facebook page, or an Instagram or LinkedIn profile, you have a reputation to protect. Paraphrasing *Alice in Wonderland*, "If you don't know where you're going, any road will take you there." Don't let someone else determine your road. Chart it yourself, for yourself.

Branding For a Company/Organization

Many of the same concepts of personal branding apply to the branding of your company or organization. What do you stand for? What's your belief system? What do you want your customers or clients to think of when they think of your business? All important questions to ask yourself. If you don't know the answers, ask someone more senior within the organization. If they can't definitively answer these questions with confidence—quickly—then you will need to begin the work of prioritizing this company-wide.

An exercise that can work really well is a pyramid system to tier your branding and business. A pyramid system is a way to look at the core of your business from the top down and bottom up. The mission is at the very top—the last portion of determining your company's branding to be completed. The first three rungs are, generally speaking, easier to quickly reach a consensus on. But the *values* are arguably the most important aspect of branding for an organization and the one you likely will spend the most time working on.

So, how do you figure out the values of your organization? As a first step, organize a meeting with a handful of top executives within the organization. Tell them that as part of building out a successful communications strategy, with the end goal of securing earned media, it is *essential* that you all are aligned on the company's values. The values, and subsequently the mission, will be the driving force behind all of your messaging that you communicate with the media, and also with your customers, clients, and stakeholders.

In the interest of leading a productive meeting, it may be helpful to lay the groundwork of the work you are doing. Explain to them what you intend to discuss and focus on. Highlight what you hope to get from the meeting as well.

Here are some questions that you can think about asking as you lead the meeting, which really should be thought of as a brainstorm:

Internal:

- Why do you like working here? Why do you think others enjoy working here?
- What makes our workplace culture unique?
- What makes you proud to work here?
- What are the weaknesses within our organization?

External:

- What value do we bring to our clients/customers?
- What do we do better than anyone else?
- How would you describe our business to those outside the organization?
- Who are we?

I'd recommend after this meeting creating a Google document where all of these values live. Once approved by senior management, it's important that they live in a central shared drive where all employees have access to understanding the company values—and, most importantly, these values must be communicated to all new staff when they first begin at the company. It's so important that, as early as possible, staff are able to understand and begin absorbing the company values.

Writing a Mission Statement

Now comes the fun part! Now, you need to take the key values/takeaways from your values brainstorm and turn them into a mission statement.

What is a Mission Statement?

According to Oxford Reference's definition, a mission statement is "a formal summary of the aims and values of a company, organization, or individual."[7] Think of it as a concise explanation of your organization's reason for existence. What is your purpose, and what is your overall intention? These should be the overarching questions you keep asking yourself as you set out to write the statement. Keep in mind that this mission statement—which will likely (or should) live on your website, and/or in any marketing materials—serves to communicate the purpose and direction of the company to employees, customers, and any other important stakeholders. That's a lot of interested parties that you need to make sure are all represented in this statement.

You can break down a mission statement into three core tenets:

1 Who is your key audience? Who are the stakeholders you're trying to reach with this statement? Keep in mind, it likely will be multiple audiences, i.e. your staff, your customer base, perhaps investors, or other partners.

2 Your contribution: How are you bringing value to these key stakeholders? What is their ROI should they choose to work with you?

3 Distinction: What makes your company the best?

You can now begin to write the statement. Here are a few things to keep in mind as you start:

- Start by explaining your company's product or service offering.
- Identify the company's core values and then connect how those values align with your company's offerings.
- Think long-term. A mission statement should encapsulate your company's current purpose and intention, but should also be reflective of future goals/growth of the business.
- Keep it short. A mission statement should be just a few sentences— no longer than a short paragraph.

How Does This Connect to PR?

Now that you have your company values and your mission statement complete, let's revert back to your primary objective—getting great PR for your company!

The main objective here is to secure *earned media*, which we know will happen by pitching to real reporters and members of the media. However, there is a lot of groundwork to be laid out *prior* to pitching. We'll get much more into this in later chapters, but for now here are some simple steps to take/keep in mind.

The first thing, the very first thing, a reporter or member of the media will do upon receiving a pitch from you is to visit your company's website and social media channels. It is really important that all of the messaging, branding, values, and mission you've just spent so much time creating and fine-tuning are easily communicated on your company's external facing channels. If your company's website doesn't have an "About" tab, create one! This is the perfect spot for you to work with your web design team to make sure this verbiage is housed. Likewise, it might make sense for you to "pin" back to this tab on your website on your various social media channels. The purpose of all of this is to make it as *easy as possible* for a journalist to understand what it is—exactly—that your company does, and what the value is. Once a journalist can quickly assess your line of work, he or she can begin their job of figuring out if there's a story there that will make sense to share with the public.

Next, maintain your brand. Share on social, or on your website or marketing materials, key "wins" that exemplify your values or mission. For example, if you land a new client that is perfectly aligned with your future goals, share that news and add a line that reverts back to your values. Or, if you make a new hire who is bringing a unique aspect to the company that is in line with your mission, create a social post on it! Share company news that identifies new offerings as well. And remember to think as a thought leader (more on that later) and create blog posts or op-eds on mainstream news in which your founder or CEO has a unique opinion to share, but can also weave the values of your own company into the piece.

Remember that branding is connecting with your audience. These days, especially amongst younger consumers, that connection is *even more important* than the transaction itself. Meaning: consumers these days want to feel a part of something. They want to support brands that are doing good in this world, whether that's through diversity, equity and inclusion (DEI), environmental, social and corporate governance (ESG), or other kinds of efforts. Case in point? Look no further than TOMS Shoes, which took off after it launched the innovative, and subsequently extremely successful, initiative of donating a pair of shoes to those in need with every purchase made.

If you can make your customers or clients feel like they are a *part of something* and that their contribution to your business is contributing in an even bigger local, national, or global sense, this will lead to more dollars and cents in the long run. It will lead to happy customers. These happy customers may then create their own social posts that reflect their satisfaction with the brand, which may lead to your re-sharing those posts, which may lead to future investors taking notice of the groundswell of emotion amongst your consumers, which may lead to them investing more money, which may lead to you being able to direct the company into future endeavors that will continue to create and strengthen a community around your brand.

Branding and PR aren't fluff—you may be told this, unfortunately, numerous times by naysayers. Don't pay attention. We know that there is a real and true value in PR. We know that this takes time to create. But we also know that once we've done this hard work and can start to see the fruits of our labor, the potential for growth and ways in which we can create value for the company are limitless.

To explain even further, Patrick Hanlon, CEO and founder of Thinktopia, a global brand and strategic innovation practice for Fortune 100 companies and start-ups alike, agreed to talk with us here about the importance of branding and other critical questions to ask yourself.

EXPERT INSIGHT

Annie: How important do you think it is for a publicist to have a solid grasp of their client's brand before they start engagement?

Patrick: I think that brands in today's world, with the mix of social, digital, and traditional media, really need to have a spine that they can rely on that is the backbone of their communications. They used to call this the big idea, when advertising agencies directed the whole thing. It would concentrate around the largest media purchase which—back then, *Mad Men* era and so forth—was the television budget for advertising, right? Today, though, that budget is scoured all over the place, so there really has to be something that's very intentional and committed to what you're all about, what you mean to people, and what's the spine behind the conversation. There has to be a hard line there.

And a lot of people just jump around from TikTok to YouTube to Instagram or whatever it is, trying to drive sales and you have to be conscious of what the medium is, and that might drive how you execute, but you really need to have a central spine there that drives things. So, we like to crunch it down into a few words that people recognize and know what you're about, and people have done "Think different," "Just do it," etc., etc. But, also, I think that it helps to focus everyone's efforts, especially in communications, but it can also help drive product or services, sometimes it's reflexive.

What we try to do is crunch it down into something you can put onto a matchbox, and then when someone asks what you're doing, what you're all about, your biggest advocates hopefully are your employees, your coworkers, the people inside the company. People talk about brands being inside out, because if the people inside your organization don't believe in what they're doing, they're certainly not going to be able to sell to anyone on the outside, right? So, it starts inside.

When you're at an event or a party or something, people ask, "What are you doing?" It's nice to have a couple words that sum it up instead of saying, "You know, I work at XYZ co." "Well, what do they do?" And who cares, right?

The second thing is, in addition to the matchbox, you know, is a couple sentences that describe what it is, what the hell you do. And you can quote me. So, what do you do? Why does it make a difference? Why does it matter? Most people don't really have that crunched down like that, and that's where it starts to get foggy and undisciplined.

Annie: Do you have a recommendation of some simple steps that somebody in that position can take to try to get to the core of their company's brand?

Patrick: If you look at brands as belief systems—what do you believe in? Defining what you believe in, and why it makes a difference in the world. Because the number one rule of marketing communications is that nobody cares, and it's our job to help make them care. No matter what media you're in, we're trying to either make them care because we want to create sales or we want to make them care so that we have meaningful work. That's the number one thing—is this video, TikTok, Facebook ad, Super Bowl spot going to help make people care about what we do to propel growth through sales, awareness, advocacy, build audiences?

Annie: What if somebody who's all of a sudden working in marketing or comms or PR doesn't know what the value systems are of the company? Are there specific questions that they can keep in mind if they are able to have an audience and they can run a meeting to help them get to this answer?

Patrick: The core of any leader is to have a vision. Where are we supposed to be in ten years, or five years? The core of leadership is to have a vision and then be able to reassure people that we're going to get there and here's how we're going to do it. Along with that comes that we are doing meaningful work. This is something that has become a cliché, but you have to remember that our parents grew up just having a job, which may not have been meaningful work for a lot of people. Working in an office or on an assembly line, or whatever you were doing, it might not have been meaningful. It's not always meaningful, perhaps, to work at an insurance company, for example, or a bank, and just plug away at your desk all day.

It may not seem like meaningful work, so what you really want to do is to figure out how to make that work meaningful. And we do that through communications and building a belief system for us. If you can explain to someone, here's how this idea started, here's what we believe in, here's what we're doing, here's how you know it's us, here's why what we're doing matters out in the world, this is not what we want to become, here's the leader, here's the team that's pulling all this together, then you've created this atmosphere of purpose and cooperation and intention. Really, intention and commitment are the two strongest things.

Annie: How do you take that purpose and commitment of the intention with you in your day to day or what you're doing?

Patrick: Two things: being intentional is really driven by having a mission, having a purpose, having a sense of meaning and commitment comes along with that. Once you do have a purpose and a sense of meaning, and you're driven by a vision of the future that no one else has, then you have a sense of commitment and you're willing to stay all night, if that's what it takes, just to make it happen.

Annie: What else does somebody need to know about branding in the context of PR?

Patrick: The way we look at brands is that they're belief systems, and once you create a belief system you attract others who share your beliefs. And that means building fans, building audiences, building consumers, or just people like us. In order to accomplish that, at least in the United States, people need to hear. This is coming from Edelman PR, a global PR company, and a study they did several years ago now, probably 5, 6, 7 years ago or more, but they did a global study, and in Singapore people need to hear about you in 17 different places before they are even aware that you exist. Before they can say, "Oh, I think I've heard of them," or "I think I've heard of that." In the United States, thankfully, it's only five places. So that helps.

The other metric that we use is that it takes a hundred hours to make a friend. That's according to a couple of sociologists, I thought they were out of Nebraska or Iowa or someplace like that, but you can Google that. It takes a hundred hours, so five places, a hundred hours, that gives you some kind of sense of scope and scale for where not just PR goes, but everything across social, digital, and traditional media.

I usually think of PR as being in traditional media, but in fact it's probably across all three, depending what you're doing. If you're posting on Instagram, that's social, but if you're doing a PR release, news release, that's a traditional release, that would be traditional. We're kind of spread.

I really think that PR is one of the crucial driving forces in communications today, because nobody believes in advertising anymore. We run from advertising. That's important because 20 years ago that was the driving force. People pulled back on that as society and communications have changed, and the others are all splintered channels.

So, PR really has an opportunity, and is a major driver because we do spread across all things. We could be creating a documentary, we could be creating an event, we could be getting people on news programs. We could be pulling people, shooting across all the media. PR has become a crucial piece of communications and has taken up the slack from all the other things, pulling it all together.

It's important to remember that it is a process. Rome was not built in a day, after all. Perception takes time. It's going to require hard work and determination for a company or a product to earn media placement. But, remember, it's better to take time and do it correctly than to rush through the process and fail.

Now, we've come to a deeper understanding of PR's crucial role in building successful brands. It's what makes a company or brand visible and memorable, even amidst a sea of competitors. But, despite its importance, the value of PR is often difficult to measure. Its impact is qualitative rather than quantitative, and it takes a skilled practitioner to execute it effectively.

As we delve deeper into the nuances of PR, it becomes clear that there are many misconceptions about what it is and what it isn't. It's not marketing, advertising, social media, or content creation, although it may be a component of these broader marketing strategies. Rather, PR is the art of maintaining a favorable public image through earned media. It's about telling your company's story in a way that captures the hearts and minds of your target audience.

The Three Spheres of Influence in Media

02

When it comes to the media, there are three big spheres of influence: print, digital, and broadcast outlets. In later chapters, we'll get into social media, advertising, and other non-traditional forms of media. But when speaking about earned media these three remain the most influential.

Print

Print, from an historical context, was the most influential—and, at one point, the only—form of media. In a time before TV, and of course, the internet, newspapers were *the* way people got their news and thus, how opinions were shaped … so much so that many papers had a morning *and* an evening edition. Think about it: there used to be no other form of news or media beyond those newspapers.

But newspapers have seen a drastic decline in recent decades.[1] Why? With the rise of the internet, information is readily available at our fingertips. However, the most-read newspapers—such as *The Times*, *New York Times*, and *Wall Street Journal*—will, in all likelihood, never die out because of their cultural importance in society.

Even still, seeing your client featured in print has a certain cachet that can't be replicated by other forms of traditional media. And if you land a cover story you've likely earned yourself a client for life.

You can think of the modern-day definition of "print," in the context of PR, as anything you can hold in your hands. Whether it be a newspaper, a magazine, a pamphlet, or newsletter, these all constitute print.

Although print used to be the *only* form of news media today, it's probably the least-coveted. Let me explain.

In today's world, news moves faster than ever before. Stories are changing and evolving, it feels like, every single minute. So it's more difficult for print outlets to stay on top of the news and to report stories in a manner that will still be timely by the time they put the paper to bed and customers purchase it the next morning.

Another reason why print is not as desirable as other forms of media is because the readership is often not as high as digital counterparts.[2] We all live on our phones and computers, so, naturally, the digital counterparts would receive a much higher readership.

Lastly, if we're comparing print and digital, you can't, of course, have a hyperlink in a printed article. And hyperlinks are *super* important when it comes to PR and pitching—more on that below.

However, print *does* elevate the brand in a way that feels very highbrow. Pretty much all of the time, a story that's in print will *also* have the digital component. But taking that clipping and showing it off to the world has a cachet you simply can't replicate online.

My favorite print story is for our former clients, real estate brokers Tom Postilio and Mickey Conlon. A longtime partnership, both in work and love, they had decided to tie the knot. Former performers, their intimate guest list was A-list and had the cachet of old-world New York.

We pitched it to the "Weddings" section of the *New York Times* and they loved it, agreeing to send a photographer. It wound up being the lead wedding in the section and to quote Tom and Mickey: "It was the best piece of press we've ever gotten"… and they had already gotten quite a bit of press at that point.

When we think of print, we also think of magazines. Magazines, much like newspapers, have also been deeply crippled by the advent of the internet, with many staple magazine shuttering over recent decades. However, many of the big ones still remain such as *Vogue*, *Elle*, and *Cosmopolitan*, and getting "in-book" is still a thrill for us publicists.

Case in point, one of our clients at my organization, Pace Public Relations, is Auvere, a 24-karat direct-to-consumer gold jewelry brand. Their pieces are beautiful and high-end. After several years, we had worked with them to develop their relationship with *Vogue*. In the world of fashion, *Vogue* is and will likely ever remain the holy grail of print media placements. We were able to get Auvere and their founder, Gina Love, in front of one of *Vogue*'s stylists. As is customary with jewelry pitching and placement, we had thought (hoped) that one of the pieces would be seen on a model in-book (inside the magazine). It was a great surprise when we saw the cover—yes, the cover—and Poet Laureate Amanda Gorman was wearing Auvere gold cuff earrings in her hair! The stylists were so creative in their positioning of the jewelry… and the response was overwhelming.

Types of Earned Print Media

Daily Newspapers

This shouldn't need too much of an explanation, and hopefully you all are familiar with daily newspapers. There are two types—national and regional.

National daily newspapers are those that have a circulation throughout an entire country. For the United States, that means newspapers are sold in each state and in Canada as well; some of the most recognizable national daily newspapers are the *New York Times*, *USA Today*, *Wall Street Journal*, *NY Post*, *LA Times*, etc.

Regional, or local, newspapers are circulated only in that particular city or surrounding area. Essentially, while they may cover major national news, and likely do, the only people who are buying and reading those papers, for the most part, live in the immediate area.

For the most part, national and regional newspapers all have the same or similar sections. Each of these represents an opportunity for you to pursue an earned media placement. It's your job as the PR professional to research, read, and get to know the reporters at these newspapers so you can identify opportunities, pitch, and hopefully place your corporation or clients there.

National News

The country's biggest stories of the day appear in the first section of all of the national newspapers and in many regional papers as well. These stories tend to deal with government, politics, natural disasters or severe weather, major travel disruptions or criminal cases that have captivated the country.

When thinking about pitching reporters who work on the National News desk, you need to be extremely careful in your approach. Typically speaking, unless you have a client who is a legitimate expert in one of these fields, with years of relevant experience and regarded as a leading voice in their particular industry, you likely will not have many, or any, opportunities to pitch these reporters.

However, if you do have a client or CEO you're working with who has relevant experience in these industries and you are pitching her or him to your local daily newspaper, you may have a real shot at getting them in an upcoming story. An example could include if your company's CEO was previously a member of Congress and now runs a political nonprofit. It would behoove you to develop a relationship with the political reporter on the national desk at your city's local newspaper. I would position your client as an expert who is available for commentary on day-of or breaking news stories. A strong tactic for getting this off the ground is to email the reporter saying something along the lines of:

> I'm familiar with your work and know that covering [*insert topic*] is your beat. I work with [*CEO name*] who was previously a member of Congress and now runs a local political nonprofit. He read the article you wrote today on [*insert subject*] and has this to say: [*provide excellent and compelling talking points*]. We'd love to invite you to come by our offices so we can meet and hopefully become a resource to you in your reporting in the future when you need expert voices to pitch.

Chances are high that you will develop a relationship this way.

International News

These are less common, but all major national newspapers have an international news section, while most regional papers do not. In the case where a paper does not have an international section, they will include relevant news from abroad in the first section, alongside national news.

These stories generally speaking are of an extremely large magnitude. For example, coverage of the Russia–Ukraine war would fit into this section. The same 'rules' of pitching apply—if you're working with a CEO or a client who had very relevant and legitimate experience in international affairs, try to establish a relationship with the most appropriate reporter in this section so you can begin to pitch her or him as a subject matter expert.

Local News

This should, again, be fairly self-explanatory, but local news for a national newspaper means the biggest news in the region in which the newspaper is based. For example, the *New York Times* is based in New York. So they have a "Metropolitan" section in which they cover NYC-area news stories. The *LA Times* has a section called "California News" where they cover the biggest stories in the state.

Regional papers such as the *Cincinnati Enquirer* do in fact have a "Local News" section, as the first portion of the paper is dedicated to national and international news. Some local papers will even have sections that are more specifically narrowed down by county or various areas. It is up to you to specifically ascertain whether each section is relevant for the company, client or CEO you are trying to secure earned media coverage for.

Generally speaking, local news is the easiest of all the sections of a paper to secure coverage in. Local news is not competitive—meaning the local news reporters *want* you to pitch them—they are likely looking for stories to write about and you could really help them by serving them up a great story.

Examples of local news stories that tend to resonate with reporters are store openings; and marches, rallies, or events that will draw a big crowd. Beyond that, "feel-good" stories tend to be a big hit. Many regional papers have a section about "hometown heroes" or something along those lines. Local news focuses on the people who live and work in the area—but, as always, do your research and make sure you have a good idea of the types of stories the section you're trying to pitch typically writes about. Research is key and will inform you and guide you into the best possible results.

Sports

Arguably the most popular section of all newspapers, the national sports section will cover the biggest games from the night before, along with any news of trades or deals being made. Local news will cover the local sports teams and get granular with various articles about key team members or aspects of the team. The only opportunity you would have to pitch the sports section is if your company works in the sports industry or has some ties to a local or national team.

Entertainment

The entertainment section is reserved for news from Hollywood and about celebrities. Typically, these types of stories actually are a good opportunity for certain types of publicists to secure earned media coverage. This is mostly because the stories tend to be a bit lighter in terms of the tone, and the topic is less serious. For example, a lead story in any given entertainment section may be about a celebrity divorce. If you work in-house running PR at a law firm, you may have a big opportunity there to have one of your lawyers weigh in and opine on the celebrity divorce du jour. Another big opportunity I've seen over the years when it comes to entertainment news is that of image and reputation. Certainly, many publicists themselves can qualify for this—but it's something to keep in mind for those you're representing.

Opinion

In Chapter 6 we'll get into thought leadership, in which op-eds are the main component. But the "Opinion" section of each newspaper is the portion where having a point of view is encouraged. This is absolutely the most fruitful portion of a newspaper where you can source opportunities for your client, as op-ed submissions are open each and every day.

Magazines

The magazine industry, like the newspaper industry, has taken a huge hit in recent decades. The early aughts were the heyday for the magazine industry, when sales and circulation were at their highest. You may remember a time when you'd go to the beach on the weekend and every group would have a handful of magazines to pore over and gossip about while sunning themselves. You may remember going to the nail salon, where the selection of magazines was always current and in demand.

Many of these magazines were what we refer to as the "celebrity weeklies." Think of *US Weekly*, *In Touch*, *Life & Style*, *People*, etc. While most of these are still in print today, their circulation has taken a dramatic hit and their cultural relevance isn't the same anymore—thanks to the internet.

I'm of an age where I remember when Perez Hilton came on the scene. It was a game changer. I remember thinking, "You mean, this page publishes new information several times a day?! Yes, please!"

There was no way that weekly, print gossip rags could keep up with this. In time, they each created their own website and primarily deliver their news and collect their revenue via ads online, as versus print. But in the early 2000s what those celeb weeklies were offering was something special, unique, and in-demand. It was before we all had smartphones at our fingertips. Those celeb weeklies were the only way we could get celebrity gossip!

Then, the internet happened. And everything changed. But as of today the following types of magazines are still in existence.

Monthly

Monthly magazines have diminished in circulation as have newspapers—but many of the most popular magazines are still in production and in demand. Most monthly magazines are women's or fashion/beauty oriented. A sampling includes *Vogue*, *Allure*, *Glamour*, *W*. Another industry that does well with monthly magazines includes shelter publications—a fancy word for housing pubs. Think of *Real Simple*, *Architectural Digest*, *Martha Stewart Living*, etc. While there are many, many other industries that have monthly publications, these are the most common.

The most important thing to remember when pitching a monthly magazine, besides all the aspects we have already discussed (research, finding the best reporter, appropriate follow-up) is the deadlines, which are considered long-lead. Each monthly magazine is "put to bed"—the unofficial term for closing out each issue—several months in advance of when that issue ever hits the newsstands. In most cases you can safely assume that is four months prior to the issue date, meaning, if you want to pitch the September issue of *Vogue* you can rest assured that they are closing that issue—meaning, they are not accepting new pitches or making any changes—past May. However, just because that is the month that they close the magazine doesn't mean you should wait until May to pitch. You should do so one to two months prior—which, I know, seems like a crazy long lead-time—but the reporters and editors you're pitching will truly appreciate that you "get it."

Getting 'in-book' at one of the major, mainstream national magazines is still considered a huge win—those pages are coveted and limited. People still read the printed versions of *Vogue* and *Vanity Fair* and they are still influential. It's not easy to get your clients featured in them—but if you have an appropriate client to pitch and you do your research to pitch appropriately it can truly help your client, and your career.

Weekly

Weekly print magazines are, generally speaking, broken into two categories: those of a more serious nature such as *Time*, *US News & World Report*, the *New Yorker*, etc.; and entertainment publications such as *People*, *US Weekly*, *In Touch*, etc.

For weekly publications, they are more or less a condensed version of what already lives on their website. But there is still a demand for the actual physical copy, which is why they are still being printed and published. For the celebrity magazines, they are chock-full of photographs of celebrities that readers love looking at… the less to actually *read*, the better. For the more serious weekly publications, oftentimes, it's a ritual, wherein readers have a subscription and read through the magazine each week to stay educated on the most important issues of the day.

In each instance, there are opportunities to position your clients, mostly, as subject matter experts to offer up quotes with insights and analysis on the stories being written.

Trade Publications

Trade publications are industry-specific periodicals that have a print component either monthly or quarterly, generally speaking. Much the same as the aforementioned print publications, most trade outlets have a digital component wherein new articles are published regularly. The print version of the trade publications allows the reporters to expand upon the original articles and offer a lengthier, more comprehensive story.

Digital

The internet changed the world as we know it, and that of course, applies to PR and our practice.

Today, digital is probably the most universally requested form of media coverage a client will ask for. To start, let's explore a little what digital means.

Digital media refers to major publications, including newspapers, magazines, and television networks, having their content available online. This content can include articles, videos, audio recordings, images, and interactive features, and is accessible through the internet using a web browser or mobile device. The shift towards digital media has allowed these traditional media outlets to reach a wider audience and engage with their readers and viewers in new and innovative ways. Additionally, digital media provides a more dynamic and immediate experience compared to traditional print publications, allowing for real-time updates and interactive features such as comments and social media integration.

The reasons client want this exposure are simple. First, the very easy to obtain metrics on how many times the article was not only read, but then subsequently shared via social media. You can't really do that with print. You can request circulation numbers, of course, but in the print form it's actually impossible to tell how many people read the exact article you had your client featured in. With a digital article you can immediately tell, most of the time—right on the page—how many views or "clicks" the piece had. This is primarily used as an indicator which drives advertising dollars for that particular reporter or outlet—but it also lets you know how many readers read that piece.

Second, the link-back to the client's home page, or product page, is highly coveted. Again, the reason comes down to tracking. When you include a hyperlink in an article, SEO whizzes can, quite easily, figure out how many people have clicked through to your client's home page via that one specific article.[3] In a world of PR where tracking is really difficult, digital articles with hyperlinks provide us with some of the best metrics out there to measure our work.

Now, let's define the digital space.

Digital is the term that those of us in the PR field use to describe any form of coverage that is online. Digital, when you combine it with the larger field of marketing and advertising, can mean a lot of different things. It can mean social media, influencer marketing, online ads (meaning banner ads, pop-up videos, and a lot else).

But when it comes to earned media coverage, there are only a few opportunities to pitch.

Websites

The overwhelming majority of the time, when you are pitching to digital outlets, you will be pitching to reporters who write for and file stories on their media outlet's website.

The tactics for pitching are exactly the same as pitching print media, except for two major differences.

First, the rate of stories being published digitally, compared to print, is much, much higher. Many print reporters don't get a piece in each daily edition. Many don't get a piece in each week. Some are happy if they get one piece in per month. On the other hand, digital reporters are filing, sometimes, six stories *per day*. What this means is that there is a real opportunity for you to develop a relationship with someone who is constantly churning out new articles.

Second, there are countless websites that would "count" as earned media coverage that do not have a print component. Think of, for example, Insider or Politico or Perez Hilton. These are just three examples out of countless digital earned media opportunities. So what does this mean? In the most basic sense, it means that these sites may not adhere to the same set of journalistic guidelines as a national newspaper. Translation: the stories may be more salacious or written with a non-objective tone. This is fine, but it's important for you to be aware of.

I'll share an example. The FTX crypto bungle was a big story that had news outlets scrambling and then filing numerous stories over the course of many months. Insider (formerly known as Business Insider) filed a story after obtaining bankruptcy documents with this headline: "FTX spent nearly $7 million on food and over $15 million on luxury Bahamian hotels in just 9 months, court documents show."[4] A national newspaper would likely not choose such a direct headline. Instead they may say something along the lines of "FTX court documents signal gross negligence," leaving the reader to uncover details within the article.

An important aspect of your job, as you attempt to secure earned media coverage for your corporation or your clients, is to become an expert in the media. Working with a news site that some consider to be salacious may not be an issue for your CEO. But what will be an issue is if you don't prep your CEO properly prior to the interview. Prepping takes work on your part—you need to read several past articles from the reporter you're working with. You need to search within the site for the subject area to read several *other* articles—not written by the specific reporter you're working with—so you can get a sense of how they report on the subject. Lastly, you should actually spend some time thinking about what a likely subject line for the forthcoming article would be—and run that by your CEO. Let her or him know that, in your extensive research into the outlet, you've noticed some patterns and he or she can expect to be included in an article with this anticipated headline. If he or she is fine with it then move forward. But if you sense trepidation from your CEO, you need to carefully reconsider if this is a good idea or not.

When you're first pitching reporters, it may seem like every piece of press is the most amazing opportunity you've ever come across in your whole entire life! But you need to try to tamp down on your excitement so you can logically think through whether or not that is actually true. You need to ask yourself—will this article help my company, my CEO or my client achieve their goals? If the answer is yes, then move forward. But if you have doubts, reconsider. Talk to colleagues. Think it through and try to map it out. It's much easier to avoid a crisis *before* it happens than to try to fix one after.

Crisis Communications

Speaking of crises… if and when you work with someone in the public eye, you do open yourself up to potential media crises. Most of the time, this will not even be something on your radar. But, there are times when a CEO missteps, and you may be called upon to "fix" the situation.

The number one piece of advice I can give about avoiding a crisis or negative articles for your client is to stop them before they occur. How do you do that? By having as much access as you can to the C-suite. This may be difficult… in fact, for many of you who work at larger corporations, this may be a notoriously difficult aspect of your job. In recent years, many companies have adopted a "flatter" structure, in which access to the CEO and C-suite is much easier and normalized as a part of the company culture. Gone are the days where the Continental Airlines CEO of the 1990s locked the door to the C-suite floor so other colleagues couldn't get in.

That said, it may still prove difficult for you to have access to key moves being made by the CEO. Of course, you don't need to know about all the major decisions… but for those decisions that even *could* have a negative connotation, you absolutely should have a seat at the table to voice your opinion.

Let's take the example of Vishal Garg, the former CEO of Better.com, who in March of 2022 laid off 900 employees… over Zoom. As Forbes describes it, it was a "cold, awkward one-way video announcement."[5]

I would hope that even if you're reading this book and have absolutely zero PR experience you would find this approach just awful. Who does that?! The backlash was crazy terrible for this CEO and the company—as it should have been—and many were very quick to judge and blame the PR team. But hear me out on why they should not be to blame for this.

Unless the "PR team" at Better.com had literally zero experience and not one functioning brain amongst all of them, there is just absolutely no way that anyone who calls themselves a publicist would have allowed such a horrendous act to occur. So what I think likely happened—and what I think happens in almost all crises where the CEO makes a really boneheaded mistake—is that the PR team actually did, in fact, say "This is not a good idea" but the CEO went ahead with it anyway. It's not a hard and fast rule, but most CEOs can be really challenging to work with, insofar as they may have massive egos. That's OK—that's probably part of the reason why they are so successful.

But, unfortunately, most CEOs view their publicist or communications team as essential *only when* there is an issue or a crisis. Some actually think they don't even deserve to be on the payroll—but think of PR as a necessary evil. How wrong they are!

If Garg's lead publicist had been able to sit in on the planning meetings surrounding the company's plan for a mass layoff, surely he or she would have advised them to not conduct the firings over a one-way Zoom video! We can immediately think of better options—in person, for one. Individualized, for another. In small groups, for another. Garg's team swung back a little, saying that the company had moved to a remote-only workforce, so delivering this news over Zoom made sense.

Fine—I can (maybe) get behind this. But to 900 people, all at once, who were completely blindsided… and unable to respond, due to the fact that it was a one-way only Zoom? Unacceptable. At the bare minimum, Garg and/or the HR team and direct managers should have conducted individual or departmental layoffs so as to not engender the feelings of bad will that most certainly did arise.

Newsletters

There are obviously many different types of newsletters that exist. Many companies or organizations have them—my firm does one that we put out twice per year. We use it as a mechanism for staying in touch with our former and current clients, prospective clients, members of the media and other "friends" of the agency. We use it as a marketing tool—and this may be something that, in your role in PR, you endeavor to create.

But there are earned media opportunities in the newsletters that media outlets put out. Even major national newspaper and digital news, culture, or lifestyle website puts out a newsletter—which offers opportunities for your clients to be featured that are not found within the digital version of the outlet (the website).

It's up to you to, again, do your research. Spend time on the websites that are of value to you and your client and you should be able to fairly quickly figure out how to sign up for various e-newsletters. The only way you'll be able to deduce which newsletters are right for your client, and then which ones have opportunities for your clients, is to sign up for them and read them. Do this for a few weeks and you'll be able to have gathered enough information to start researching who is the editor of each newsletter and how you can best go about approaching that editor to start a conversation.

Another pro-tip is, after you secure an interview for your client in the website, ask the reporter you've been working with if this story is planning to be featured in their newsletter. If you have developed a somewhat friendly relationship with the reporter, you might be able to casually ask what the process is for determining which stories get selected for the newsletters. If you're working with a more junior reporter, this may prompt her or him to push for your story's inclusion in the newsletter. Either way, it continues to demonstrate to the journalist that you know your stuff and are taking seriously the role of PR professional.

Social Media

In Chapter 9 we'll absolutely get into social media tactics as an area in which PR professionals are beginning to spend more time in growing their career. But in terms of earned media and elongating the impact of your digital press hits, there are some tactics you can implement within the pitching process.

First and foremost—follow the digital media outlet, the reporter, and the section (if it's on social media. For example, if you're working on a story that will be included in the *New York Times* "Style" section, follow the *New York Times* "Style" section!). Ideally, you would have done this *prior* to pitching, as a mechanism for educating yourself on the reporter and outlet you're pitching. But if you haven't, now is definitely the moment.

Follow all of the social platforms the outlet is on, but concentrate on whichever of the platforms the outlet has the most followers and the most engagement. You're doing this so that you can—at the appropriate time—ask if your client's story will be featured on any of their social platforms. And, if you're able to make an informed suggestion of which platform would make the most sense for this particular story—even better.

Spend some time identifying the tone or voice that's captured on the outlet's social media. If photographs play a big role, you should immediately start thinking about what visual assets you can offer up to the reporter, with this in mind. Video is even better, if any exists.

The other thing that could help get your client's story featured on social is if your client has a large social presence. The goals of social media are to grow followers and increase engagement. If your client has 20,000 followers on Instagram, and the media outlet's social media manager sees this—and sees that you have good engagement—this would definitely help in terms of tipping the scales of whether or not you could get the social post for your client.

If the media outlet chooses to *not* share your client's story on their social media, don't fret. This is your opportunity to either create a fantastic social media post and strategy, or to work with whoever oversees social media at your company.

Social media is subjective so there is no exact right or wrong way to go about it. What you can control and do correctly is to make sure you are tagging the appropriate accounts and adding the appropriate hashtags. You always want to tag in your post the media outlet, the section, and the reporter. You want to (naturally) be very compli-mentary in your post and call out how great it was to work with the reporter.

Remember that one story doesn't *necessarily* equate to only social post on your part. You could do an Instagram grid post—but also break it down into several stories for Instagram. The same rules apply—tag and hashtag as much as you can. You likely should also do at least one native post for each social media platform your company is on (Twitter, Instagram, TikTok, Facebook, LinkedIn, etc.).

Broadcast

When broadcast television came on the scene, it was a real game changer. Back in the 1950s, it was such a novel concept for TV watchers to see newscasters from the comfort of their living rooms; it forever changed how we consume media.

Pretty much from the onset, Americans have had a love affair with TV. CNN's launch in 1980 as the first 24/7 cable news network was another watershed moment. In 2007 streaming capabilities were introduced, and now we could watch live TV on our devices.

I'm biased, mostly because I spent the first decade of my career as a TV news producer, but I still believe TV is king when it comes to any media platform. To be successful in almost any PR campaign, you need to work with all media—including print and digital, and radio and podcasts, too—but nothing can move the needle like TV can (when done correctly).

The main reason for this is the very large audience that the networks pull in. For example, *Good Morning America* averages around three million viewers each morning. Think about that—if you get your client featured on this program, millions of people will be watching that segment—and likely purchasing or googling whatever it is you're selling or promoting. While the *New York Times* has more than 100 million subscribers—a huge number—it's impossible to know how many people are actually *reading* the articles in the print edition. When you get your client on TV, you likely have a very captive audience—which means you're going to feel the impact of the piece airing.

The value of a national morning show can also be calculated when you compare it to what a commercial would cost during the show's airtime. According to Fast Capital 360, a 30-second commercial that airs nationally costs several hundred thousand dollars.[6] Think about that! Most TV segments are around three or four minutes long—if you secure a national TV spot for your client the ad dollar equivalent could be around a million dollars! (Time to ask for a raise!)

Let's go through the various types of broadcast media so that you can start to familiarize yourself with the industry and start figuring out which networks and shows make the most sense for you to start pitching.

National TV

National TV is anything that—you guessed it—airs nationally. These networks have a much larger reach than a streaming platform or a local TV station. Securing your client on a national network will not only—likely—help your client's bottom line and to get their message across, but it will also immediately put them on the national stage, meaning their credibility and legitimacy will grow as a result. Let's get into the types of national TV that offer opportunities for earned media coverage (i.e., we won't be discussing sitcoms or judge shows).

National Network News

The major network news stations in the United States are ABC, CBS, and NBC. Fox, the CW and a few others are considered national news as well, but they don't have the reach that the big three do. Each of the three major networks has a morning show, an evening news-cast, a Sunday program and one or more news magazine style shows, allowing for opportunities to pitch your clients and secure earned media coverage.

National morning shows are amongst the most coveted broadcast interviews you could secure for a client. There are a few ways you could go about pitching your client for earned media coverage to a morning show. The first would be a one-on-one interview, on-set or remote. This is the hardest type of interview to secure on a morning show, mostly because these interviews are reserved for newsmakers, politicians, celebrities, and bold-faced names. It's not impossible to secure this type of interview for your client—but it is difficult.

Next is inclusion in a taped package. This would be an opportunity for your client to offer up a sound bite that would be included in the piece. And finally, if your client is a physical product, there are oftentimes segments in which the show's contributor or another guest will outline for the viewers at home a roundup of products. This is an amazing type of segment to have your client featured in, for the exposure. Currently, national morning shows that air product segments cut deals with the product directly so that they can sell a certain amount via their own website. It's important you understand this *prior* to pitching your company's product for inclusion in a product segment. The network will actually purchase, directly from your client, a set number of products—but there is a *lot* of negotiating during this process, wherein, typically, the show wants to have a very advantageous cut of the products sold via their live show or subsequently on their website. Each brand must decide for themselves if this is going to make sense or not. For those with deeper pockets, it may make sense because the overall exposure may be more valuable than breaking even on a few hundred units that are needed for this opportunity. For smaller brands, though, where the margins are much tighter, these types of opportunities may not make sense for you to engage in, right at this exact moment.

To get your client featured on a national morning show you really do need to watch the show. Set your DVRs or go online and review segments each day. This research will inform you of the best course of action to take when pitching for an earned media placement.

Talk Shows

Long gone is the golden heyday of talk shows. I'm thinking *Oprah*, *Donahue*, *Geraldo*, *Sally Jessy Raphael*. But today there are still several very popular talk shows that offer up an incredible opportunity for clients to get featured.

The same type of bookings are applicable here as they were for the national morning shows—live one-on-one interviews, taped packages, and product placement. Today's talk shows tend to be very celebrity focused—so if you are representing someone who works in or has previously worked in the entertainment industry it will make sense for you to watch the *Kelly Clarkson Show*, or *Live! With Kelly and Ryan*, as your client may be a viable option as a talking head expert.

These morning shows all tend to do a lot when it comes to product placement as well. Keep in mind that most of these shows are filmed in front of a live studio audience—and if you are lucky enough to get the interest of the producer for a product segment what comes along with it is an audience giveaway. This is almost a certainty. Most studio audiences are around 200 seats, so you'll need to know this going into the process. Make sure you speak with the appropriate team members from your company to understand if this is realistic or not.

Reality TV

Reality TV is huge (thank you, Andy Cohen!). You may be thinking to yourself, "But how could I ever secure earned media coverage for my client on a reality TV show?" The answer is—it's not exactly simple, but there are definitely opportunities you could source.

If you think of a reality franchise, like *The Real Housewives*, in many episodes they are taking a trip somewhere and usually stay at a very nice resort. It is absolutely the work of the PR team at that resort that arranged for that stay, in exchange for the credit in the show. By credit, I do mean—yes—at the very end of the episode where the text scrolls on screen and you'll see something like "Thank you to [*name of resort*]." But I also mean when you're watching the show and they all first arrive—the camera pans to the name of the resort and holds it for a couple of seconds—that's another form of credit that was likely negotiated prior to the segment filming. Obviously, the entire show, or at least a part of it, will take place at the resort, with the reality stars hopefully having a great time. This is all so valuable for PR promotion.

Let's say you work in the food and beverage industry and your CEO is a chef. You may be able to pitch him to one of the many cooking shows out there as a judge for an upcoming episode.

The point is, when watch TV now, do so through the lens of thinking—is there an opportunity here for my client? You'll be surprised at how many times you say "yes" and how just this simple exercise can open you up to finding new opportunities.

Cable News

CNN, Fox News, and MSNBC are the big three cable news networks. CNN was the first and Fox News is the biggest, by a long shot (in terms of viewership and the key demo). Business cable networks include CNBC, Fox Business, and Bloomberg. Out of all the national TV opportunities, cable news provides the most, simply because there are more hours of programming than at other national outlets, which means more guests and segments are needed every single day.

Cable news focuses mostly on national news, with a heavy focus on politics. However, there are some international segments, and some entertainment focused news. Cable networks follow whatever are the biggest or most trending stories of the day.

As far as securing an earned media placement in TV, cable news is a great place to give it your best shot. Each hour on cable TV news averages around ten guests; multiply that by the number of hours the network is live—in some instances 20 out of 24 hours per day—and you can quickly see why this is a populous area to pitch your client.

The types of guests that tend to get booked often on cable news include political pundits, financial analysts, attorneys, medical doctors, and reporters. Most of the time, these guests are getting booked in the thought leadership/subject matter expertise vein, meaning, they are not going on to discuss whatever news is coming out of their own company or organization—they are there solely to opine on the day's news and offer up their opinion with compelling commentary.

Streaming

When most people think of streaming, they think of apps like Netflix, Amazon Prime, or Hulu, where they can watch original and other content—mostly movies or scripted TV shows.

But streaming, in the context of earned media, means mostly news coverage. Each major network has their own streaming component: NBC has Peacock; CBS has CBSN; Fox News has Fox Nation, and on and on. For the most part, these streaming platforms mimic the content and style of their national counterpart. They have their own shows with different anchors. But the essence remains the same. The viewership is not nearly as large on these streaming platforms as it is on the national scale—but they tend to be easier to secure and still come with the branded letters of the network—which is great for your client to put on their website or in their marketing materials. These streaming networks make money for the networks—some have a subscription-based model, and they all take in ad dollars.

There are some independent streaming networks as well—Cheddar TV, Yahoo! Finance, and others. Again, these streaming networks offer a softer lift when securing your first national booking.

Local TV

Each major city in the nation has its own local TV news. Most cities have several competing networks for their local news; generally speaking they are ABC, NBC, CBS, Fox, and then perhaps one or two local stations.

Local TV is a great place to go after earned media placements. Again, this requires research and time spent watching each of the networks. But many local news networks have a morning show, with the same opportunities for securing coverage as there are on the national scale. Some may offer weekend shows, which is, yet again, another fantastic opportunity for your client.

The opportunity is easier to get your client on local TV because there are likely just not as many newsworthy things happening around town as there are on the national scale. In some instances, the producers and reporters may be desperate for good stories or sources to interview for various pieces. Play to your local roots and try to make a genuine connection with reporters in your area—this will undoubtedly lead to earned media coverage.

Summary

The three spheres of influence in media—print, digital and broad-cast—are the quintessence of the ever-changing media landscape that shapes and informs public opinion. Though print held a paramount position in history as the only source of news and opinions, the advent of digital media has transformed the communication paradigm. Today, digital media is ubiquitous, and clients frequently demand its coverage for its vast reach and easy accessibility.

However, while digital media's popularity burgeons, broadcast media, especially television, remains the king of media platforms. A well-executed TV segment can move the needle of public opinion in ways that digital or print media may find hard to replicate. As public relations professionals, it is crucial to understand the strengths and limitations of each medium and craft a targeted approach that capitalizes on its unique qualities.

Moreover, the ever-evolving media landscape demands that PR professionals stay abreast of emerging trends and technologies. Social media, influencers, and podcasts present new opportunities for PR practitioners to engage with their target audience more personally. Non-traditional forms of media have enabled brands to reach audiences in ways never before possible.

Ultimately, the three spheres of influence in media represent the cornerstone of earned media, while social media, influencers, and podcasts are the new frontiers of media outreach. In navigating these mediums, PR professionals must remain flexible, adaptable, and imaginative in their approach to effective communication. The ever-changing media landscape requires an unrelenting commitment to staying informed, creative, and innovative to ensure a brand's message resonates with its intended audience.

Origin Story 03

You may have never heard of the phrase "origin story" before reading this sentence. That's OK. From now on, though, listen for it. You'll realize you were hearing it more than you ever thought.

An origin story is how you describe your company's inception, its creation. It gives the tactical, practical, logistical side of how the company or brand was born. But the best origin stories are rooted in emotion and describe the "why" behind the business.

Each brand or company has an origin story. Whether or not that origin story is written down somewhere and used in marketing materials or when delivering presentations is a different matter. But every business out there started for a reason—the origin story is just the mechanism by which we capture this reason and put it into words.

Uber's origin story is a great one.[1] The two co-founders, who were friends, were together on a trip to Paris in 2008. They found themselves on the snowy streets of Paris, unable to locate a taxi. They joked around, saying how they wished they could order a limo through an app on their phone. A year later, Uber was created.

Many brands start off with an issue that arises. The new brand aims to fix that problem or offer a solution. Away, the luggage company, which was a client of ours for years, has a similar origin story to Uber. One of the co-founders was in an airport and her luggage broke. Her phone was dying and she couldn't find a charging station. She called her friend, who became the other co-founder, saying something along the lines of, "There must be an easier way to travel. There's got to be a better way." It was that conversation that prompted the two to start Away, creating a stylish, lightweight, indestructible suitcase, with superior wheels and a built-in phone charger with battery.

It's your job as the PR professional at your organization to know the origin story of the company. There may not be one yet, or there may be one that seems thin, like it's missing aspects to it. Now is the time to press along and go deeper, getting to the heart of why and how the company started in the first place.

Creating the Origin Story

If you ask your manager or CEO, "Hey, what's our origin story?" and they look at you blankly... Houston, we've got a problem!

I jest. It's not a real problem. But it will require time and effort on your part to uncover and figure out what exactly is the origin story of the company you work at or of your client. Without knowing how they started and where they came from, your pitches may fall a little flat and may not be as impactful as you had hoped.

I've outlined here some simple steps to follow to help you to figure out and then create the origin story for your brand. Hopefully these steps will make this process as smooth and easy as possible.

1. Start With Your Own Research

I know this sounds like PR 101... because it is! But you can't jump down to number 2 (ask for an audience with your founder) without doing your own research and coming in as prepared as possible.

Researching your own company or your client *should*, in theory, be relatively easy. Obviously, start by poring over the website and reading as much as you can, looking for any info you can find on why the company was started, by whom, and when. If your founder is active on social media, particularly LinkedIn, make sure you check that out as well, as there is a potential that he or she has written posts in the past about the origin story. Make sure you search on Google and in Google News for any articles or previous pieces of press that come up that may give you clues and insights into the origin story. Last, ask your colleagues and managers if they know why the company was started and what the origin story is. This should give you enough intel to move on to the next step.

2. Ask for an Audience With Your Founder

This may need to be handled delicately, based on many different factors. Some founders are no longer that involved with the company. Some founders may not make themselves available, generally speaking, to the team, and in particular to those who may be junior or mid-level. Some of you may have no problem getting a meeting with the founder. Whatever your specific situation is, I would recommend first going to your manager for a discussion. Without having access to the founder and hearing straight from her or him on why they founded the company, your origin story is going to be flat at best and inaccurate at worst—neither of which you want. Explain how important it is for securing earned media coverage that you understand fully the *why* behind the company's creation. Appeal to your manager's senses—explain that through this meeting, you will be one step closer to securing media coverage. Let them know that, without it, your job is going to be that much more difficult.

Use these same tactics to figure out the best way to go about scheduling this meeting—should you email the founder's admin? Should you wait to run into her or him in the hallway? I can't tell you the exact way that you should go about doing this—but give it some thought. This may be the biggest internal meeting you've had to date—and you want to make sure you nail it.

3. Prepare

If you are fortunate enough to get a meeting with the founder of the company, or the founder of your client's brand, consider this a huge "win" and one not to be taken lightly. Spend time preparing for this meeting.

First, where are you meeting? In the office or in another location? Make sure if it's not in the office, you look in advance to see how far away it is so you can make sure you arrive not on time but early. The very last thing you want to do is to keep the founder waiting for you and risk having them be in a bad mood before your conversation begins.

Make sure you are dressed appropriately. Again, I realize that this may sound super basic—but these things matter. Dress professionally, but it's OK to dress in a manner that's authentic to yourself. Just make sure you look polished and professional.

Remember to look her or him in the eye when you meet and shake their hand. Too formal? It's not. They will appreciate that you are taking this meeting seriously and treating them with an appropriate amount of respect.

Set the stage. Let her or him know that you appreciate them making time for you today and that the purpose of this meeting is to be able to start a dialogue that will begin to capture the origin story of the brand. Let them know that this is a critical part of earned media outreach—it's a question that journalists may ask you and you want to be fully prepared. But also that by understanding the nuances of how the company was formed, this will help you to figure out appropriate news hooks and avenues for pitching.

Make sure you ask the founder if he or she is okay with you recording the conversation. You'll want to take notes, of course, but if you are able to record it then the pressure is off in terms of trying to capture every single word while they're talking.

Make sure you come prepared with a list of questions to ask. Your research up to this point will inform the list of questions you have prepared but here are some suggested ones that could come in handy:

- Was there a specific moment that prompted you to start this company?
- What do you remember about that exact moment that led you to having this big idea? Were you struggling with something at the time?
- After you had the idea, what did you do then? What were the next steps you took?
- How do you describe the purpose of our company?
- In 20 years, what do you hope the legacy of our brand will be?

The point of this meeting with the founder is to have a conversation. It's through relaxed conversation that you can get to the heart of what you want to hear—the real nuggets of genuine emotion from your founder. What you want is to get as personal as possible—to capture pieces of information, memories, original thoughts that you can use as you begin the next stage in this process.

When you finish the interview, thank her or him and let them know that nothing will happen without getting their approval first and that you'll be in touch shortly.

4. Write it Down

Hopefully this meeting will leave you with a ton of good information to digest. The best course of action for figuring out where to start is to identify if there was a memorable story that the founder said over and over again. Were there key phrases or terms that he said repeatedly? Were there moments when he got really passionate and super excited? These moments will give you the first taste of where you can and should begin.

Remember that everything you write must be true. You may find yourself saying, "Yeah, but if I just embellish this one little part, it would be so much sexier." Don't do it—it's a cardinal rule in PR, and should be in life. Don't lie—just tell the truth. Root your origin story in what actually happened.

Keep it simple—and this may require some editing. Many, when they first start writing an origin story, feel as though they need to include every single date when something "big" happened that led to the formation of the company. This should not be the case. You're weaving together a story, a narrative that, above all else, should hold the reader's attention. Don't get bogged down in too many details or dates.

Focus less on how it happened and more on *why* it happened. The "why" is everything in this exercise. Try to write as clearly as possible, while making it concise and compelling.

Next, identify *the* moment. In every founder's story there was a precise moment in time where the proverbial "light bulb" moment occurred. This could be a moment of inspiration for your founder. It could be the moment when an early customer actually bought into it. Whatever the exact moment was—this is the key to writing your company's origin story.

Last, use as much specific and vivid imagery as possible. In my own origin story, getting laid off unexpectedly from my job in TV news was a turning point in me starting my own business. A boring line in an origin story would read like this: Annie got laid off and decided to use that as the moment to start her company. Instead, a much more compelling way to say the same thing would be to say:

> Annie was unexpectedly laid off and found herself scared, at age 28, without a job. She did what any young woman would do—she called her mom and cried. But she quickly realized that getting laid off was the best thing that ever happened to her when a former publicist reached out to her and asked if she could help book his client on TV. That was the moment that started everything.

5. Get the Founder's Approval

Asking for *two* meetings with the founder may be pushing it. What I recommend first is running the origin story by your manager or someone else who is more senior than you are at the company. When you feel really good about the origin story, email it to your founder. Say this is just a draft and, since it's really her or his origin story, you are more than open to any and all changes. You can say that you want this process to be collaborative, and you want to be as helpful as possible.

6. Incorporate This Messaging Into Everything

The origin story is a critically important part of the lexicon of the company or brand and it should be treated as such. Make sure this messaging is incorporated into any and all important written aspects of the company—particularly your website! There should be an "About" section—make sure that the origin story is either weaved into this section or has its own stand-alone portion. It's probably a good idea to start incorporating the origin story into your marketing materials, meaning your proposals and investor decks, etc. People want to work with *people*—so by humanizing your organization, and showing off (some of) your vulnerability, it's going to create a safe space for collaboration and partnership. Make sure, if appropriate, to have the origin story, or part of it, featured on your social media.

7. Figure Out Who is Going to Communicate This Origin Story

Clearly, your founder will (hopefully) be the main person communicating the origin story of his or her own company. However, there may be others from your company who should know how to verbally communicate this—and you need to be the one in charge of facilitating this undertaking.

What I mean by that is—now is a good time to start thinking about who, from your company, *could*, potentially, be a spokesperson for the brand. Your founder, while an obvious possibility, may be shy and veer away from media opportunities or speaking publicly. It's your job to uncover this and then come up with a solution for an alternate spokesperson.

The most obvious next choice would be the CEO (or president, if your organization does not have a CEO). The CEO runs the company and therefore is a much bigger "get" for media outlets to interview. A lot of time, when you're dealing with clients, they may want to have their head of marketing, or even someone within their comms department to take the lead on earned media opportunities. If you can get the CEO, founder, or president to agree to do interviews this will make your job a heck of a lot easier. At the major national news networks, it's always going to be a more compelling interview if you can offer up the highest-ranking member of the organization to go on camera. You should convey this to your client. So much of PR is educating the client on how the media works—a lot of times, clients simply just don't know or understand the media. They may think it's perfectly fine to have their head of marketing do a live interview on CNBC. There's nothing *wrong*, per se, with this line of thinking— totally understandable. But when you start to explain the nuances of the media to them, it will just make your job easier because you'll have fewer roadblocks when dealing with clients. When you're able to explain to them that CNBC only likes to bring on CEOs of publicly-traded companies, or those with more than $1 billion assets under management, you will be able to proceed with a pitch to the producers that hopefully will be met with a booking. Once a client understands this, they won't keep asking you to book their head of marketing.

Media Training

Completing the origin story is a perfect time to start thinking about media training at your company. For those not familiar with media training, it is the process by which senior members of the organization undergo preparation to help them ace interviews. Chapter 8 goes into the mechanics of media training, but at this stage in your earned media approach you need to start thinking about who is best to represent the company.

As a place to start, if you're unfamiliar with who has previously been a spokesperson for your organization, look online. Your company's website should have a "News" section, or a quick Google or YouTube search should yield the results you're looking for.

If there are videos of various reps from the company doing on-camera interviews, watch them. Study them and critique them. Do you think they speak well on camera? Do you feel like they adequately represent the company? Are they sharing the brand's message in the best way possible?

If the answers are all "yes" then you've found your on-camera, company spokespersons. If the answer is "no" then you need to do some investigating.

As mentioned, start at the top of the company and work your way down. Generally speaking, a C-suite executive would make a good candidate as a spokesperson. Something to strongly consider is having a diverse pool of candidates to represent the brand. There are a couple of reasons behind this. First, there is so much, warranted, attention on DEI efforts within organizations of all sizes—yours shouldn't be any different. While you, presumably, do not work in HR and are not responsible for setting up or implementing those processes, you are a main conduit to the public for your organization. It's extremely important that all stakeholders see—from an external perspective—that your company is a living embodiment of DEI initiatives and that diverse choices are reflected when doing on-camera interviews.

The second reason to ensure the diversity of your representatives is because it's important to the networks you'll be pitching! In recent years, *all* of the networks have made it a priority to move away from booking mostly "old white men" and have on more women and more people of color. If you are able to reach out to a booker at a national news network with a female or minority guest, your chances will be higher of booking that person than if you were to approach that same producer with a white guy. That's just a fact.

Go one step further—make sure in your email pitch to the producers you include a headshot and bio. You may even want to call out any particularly attention-grabbing aspects from their bio, such as: "Jane Doe is the first black, female CEO of our organization."

The process of figuring out who from your organization will be a candidate for on-camera interviews, and thus media training, is one that should be able to be done fairly simply. First, start by asking either your direct report or, if you have access, the CEO who that person or persons should be. A lot of times, when we're working with clients, we like to have at least two options for pitching purposes. As I'm sure you see within your own organization, there are different facets to a company. Your CEO is likely the best person to give interviews on major company news, earnings or partnership announcements. But perhaps your chief marketing officer, who, let's say, is a female, may be the best person to discuss any new marketing or DEI initiatives your company has. If this CMO is young, or a person of color, you can easily pitch outlets that cater to those audiences as a way to expand your earned media outreach.

While we get into the tactical elements of media training in Chapter 8, you are going to want to make sure that you have identified members of your team who are willing to go on camera. Make sure they understand that *live* TV is a very real possibility. Sometimes, a person can say, "Yes, sure, I'll do TV," but then when they start to learn more, or understand how large the audience is, they may get cold feet. You'll want to be painfully obvious with them about the outlets you are pitching and all that goes into those interviews.

Make sure you identify representatives who are available on short notice to make a live TV interview happen. Someone who travels four or five days every week or is in meetings that are immovable day over day may not be the best candidate for you.

You'll want to use your intuition about who you think, naturally, speaks the clearest and in the most compelling manner. If someone is boring in real life they are likely going to be boring on camera. That's not to say that media training can't help with that—it totally can. But if you have the option of choosing between someone who is naturally charismatic versus someone who is not you're going to want to make that choice.

Once you've identified your on-camera spokespeople, and before the tactical media training begins, you'll need to make sure these folks very clearly understand the origin story and what messaging is important to the company to convey during these interviews. At Pace PR we use a new client questionnaire (see Chapter 4) that helps us to get on the same page with our clients about all aspects of PR and our work together. Aspects of the questions we ask may be salient as you move forward with your own PR work.

It's apparent the power of an origin story transcends mere marketing jargon. It is a force that connects businesses with their customers on a visceral level, one that engenders trust and fosters loyalty. An origin story is more than a tale of how a company came to be—it is a reflection of the values and beliefs that underpin the business. It provides a window on the soul of an enterprise and imbues it with a sense of purpose that resonates with customers.

But an origin story is not simply a vehicle for commerce; it is a call to action, a testament to the human spirit that drives innovation and creativity. It is a reminder that every great enterprise, every magnificent idea, started with a spark of inspiration, a flicker of hope, and a lot of hard work.

However, as with all things, the power of an origin story can be corrupted if it is not authentic. It must be true to the heart and soul of the business, a reflection of its true essence. Anything less is an affront to the intelligence of customers who can easily see through the facade.

A well-crafted origin story is more than a marketing gimmick; it is a work of art, a masterpiece that tells the story of a business, its triumphs and failures, its hopes and fears. It is a testament to the human spirit and a call to action that inspires and motivates. So, listen for the origin stories of the businesses around you and remember the power of your own story, for it is the foundation upon which your success will be built.

Setting Goals

04

One of the most valuable lessons I learned in PR came from a professor of mine when I was studying public relations in graduate school. I've already referenced this quote in Chapter 1, but I truly think of it often in my daily work and in my own professional development. She quoted the saying: "If you don't know where you're going, any road will take you there."

I think about this quote all the time, in the context of running my business, in the context of my client work and in the context of my own personal and professional development. Without knowing your goals and what you are trying to achieve, it's all for naught.

So, what are your goals? Perhaps you haven't yet thought about this question seriously. Well, it's time to do that. To start, it might be worth referring to your job description. Presumably, the goals for your role in publicizing the brand or company you work for should be mentioned in your job description. If not, it's time to take control of your own career path and start creating these goals yourself. You may be in a position where you need to advocate for yourself and your position within the company.

The high-level goal for many of you will be to secure earned media coverage for your company, brand or CEO/founder. But, why? You need to ask yourself this question, but also take the time to hopefully discuss this with your CEO/founder and other key stakeholders within this process. Ask yourself:

- Why do we need PR?
- What are we trying to accomplish?
- Who are we trying to reach?

Let's break them down one at a time.

Why Do We Need PR?

At some point, every single company will consider PR as a way to enhance their business. Most businesses will seriously consider hiring an agency to help with this. It's your job to get down to the most honest answer and assess it, by spending real time reflecting on this and then polling those whose opinions also matter in this process.

Some potential answers to this question, that you may realize or that may be verbalized to you, are as follows:

"Our competitors are getting a ton of press. We should be too!"

I get this one a *lot*. Many times, businesses won't even have PR remotely on their radar… until they see their #1 competitor in the local newspaper, or doing a TV interview, or bragging about a recent press hit on their social media feed. Then you might have a slightly perturbed boss who all of a sudden has made it her or his mission to "beat" this competitor in press coverage and media appearances.

Your boss may be this blatant. I've had clients be this explicit with me in the past. A lot of times, though, this sentiment is masked, under the guise of "it's just the smart thing to do." Either way, it is fine. It's your job to gather all of the information and use your intelligence quotient (IQ) and emotional quotient (EQ) to assess the situation.

If this does happen, you have some work to do. First, you need to determine if you agree with this decision. If you do agree with it, hopefully for non-ego-related reasons but more for the good of the company, then there's nothing to discuss—you can move forward with the rest of your goal-setting. However, if you strongly disagree with this strategy, you may want to consider pushing back with your boss.

I say "may" because each one of you will have a different relationship with your boss and different factors will be at play with regards to your current employment and career path. You're obviously interested in earning fantastic PR for your company if you are reading this book. But you may have very different ideas about how to approach PR for your company that does not involve spiting competitors.

If this is the case, then you need to lay out your argument really carefully and thoughtfully to your boss. This is where your EQ will come into play. You need to appeal to your boss to get them to sign off on your new plan. To do this, you need to always lead with intention, and that intention is to do the best work to help your current company. You could consider using language such as, "I know it bothers you when you see our competitor getting press. But you know what would bother him even more than seeing you doing an interview? *This!*" and then you can lay out your plan.

Spiting competitors should really not be a valid reason for engaging in PR efforts. If this is the direction you're pushed toward, however, then simply revert back to your job description. Surely, this reason can't be written in a formal, company job description. So, together you're going to need to come up with new KPIs and metrics to measure how well you're performing within your PR duties.

Often, your company needs PR to generate leads and sales.

This is a tricky one, because PR does not directly correlate to sales. If your boss is really pushing new sales, new customers, new clients, try your best to redirect them to marketing, direct sales, and advertising efforts. Those efforts are *much* easier to measure, therefore making them quantifiable.

PR, on the other hand, is qualitative. This means that it's *very difficult* to measure the ROI.

So, what you *can* measure with PR is views/clicks/shares. Meaning: you can easily find out the unique monthly views or viewers of the media outlet, via a subscription to Cision (more on this a little later). Many digital articles will have at the bottom the number of times the article was shared or commented on, or how many viewers read that exact article (these are for digital, not print articles, of course). But that still won't lead you to understanding how many *new sales* you've accrued as a result of the PR placement.

With advancing technology, if your company has the ability to track sales via clicks, then you will, actually, be able to tell how many new sales come via each digital article *that links back to your site.* I put this in italics to demonstrate not every digital outlet will allow you to link back to your company's website. This is purely up to the discretion of the editorial team at each news outlet.

LINK-BACK POLICIES

It's actually really important to research and to ask directly about a site's link-back policy before you set up an interview with an outlet. Why? Because you want to avoid a situation where you work so hard to set up an interview, spend time prepping and coordinating, only for them to write a great article about your company without a hyperlink to get people to your website. It's *much* easier to ask for these types of things in advance as opposed to after the fact. Journalists will usually comply, if they can, or at least be polite about it if it they cannot accommodate a request. But if you ask them after the fact, chances are they have already moved on from your particular story and are on deadline for the next thing. The power dynamic is off; they already published the story. Their job is done.

So, in advance of setting up an interview, review several articles on the outlet's site. Do they hyperlink to other companies whose CEOs they interview? Is that standard across multiple articles? Or, in your research, do you see that they never hyperlink to outside websites? If that's the case, despite a very polite ask, you may not get the hyperlink.

If this is the case, you should address it head on with your CEO before you arrange the interview. Let them know if you think this is a great opportunity and lay out your case as to why. Is it a very prominent publication? Do they get a ton of viewers? Will they promote the story on their social media channels? Is there an opportunity this article will help with your SEO/marketing/social media efforts, even without a hyperlink?

In all aspects of business and PR, it's better to get *ahead* of a situation, versus playing catch up after the fact.

For someone to want to engage in PR, there is always some level of ego involved. And that's OK. In fact, it's actually a good thing because that ego will likely drive a better interviewee, one who preps more thoroughly and is more engaged during an interview. However, you have an important job to do and that starts with using all of your institutional knowledge, and EQ, to ascertain if, in fact, your boss is the best person to represent the company in a public forum. Is the CEO well-spoken? Do they present well? Talk clearly and succinctly and with passion? Readily available?

If you are answering "yes" to these questions, then we can revert back to the previous train of thought. If there is another, more substantial benefit to your boss speaking publicly on behalf of the company, that's great. You can pivot their egotistical intentions into the greater good of the company. But if the answer is no, or you do not feel confident about her/his ability to deliver, then a conversation persuading them to pursue another route to get awareness for the company may be the best approach forward. "We need to incorporate PR into our overall marketing budget because it's an important aspect in any growing business' plan." Ding, ding, ding! This sounds like the kind of thoughtful, pragmatic approach a seasoned and skilled business leader would take. You're off to a good start if this is the answer you've received.

What Are We Trying to Accomplish?

Getting Granular

Now that you've assessed the reasoning behind PR implementation, the next step is to write down your goals and set up a system wherein you can measure KPIs and your successes.

What Are We Trying to Accomplish?

Before you launch into a PR campaign, you need to understand the goals and your objectives. This can best be done by using a questionnaire that you can circulate to your C-suite or client contact.

New Client Questionnaire

First, start with the overarching goal of the company. Most companies level-set each year and set a new goal within their operating plan. If you don't have access to your company's operating plan, request it immediately.

Second, write down what the overarching goal is for PR engagement, i.e., "To increase awareness of the brand through an ongoing drumbeat of national media placements" or "To secure multiple TV interviews around the launch of [*insert anything*] as a way to enhance our overall marketing plans."

At my agency, an immediate step we take when we onboard a new client is to have them fill out our new client questionnaire. This is a way for us to get to know the client really, but also to hear in their own words what their goals are.

Below, I've provided an example of a new client questionnaire. For each new client, these questions can and should be personalized, but you can use this as a starting point for your next project.

NEW CLIENT QUESTIONNAIRE

Client Coordination

1 Is a biweekly call feasible for you, the liaison, and/or your team? We recommend a scheduled call every two weeks, with regular and consistent updates over email or a quick less formal phone call in the period between.

2 Who is your spokesperson? If many, please list out each spokesperson and their topics/areas of expertise.

3 What topics in the media are you/your spokespeople most comfortable speaking on?

4 What forms of media are you most comfortable with (e.g., print, TV, radio)?

5 If a story broke at a moment's notice in your well of expertise, would you be able to provide talking points as soon as possible?

6 Who is the best liaison for us to be in touch with if we have questions that need to be answered?

7 Can you give us an idea of your calendar for the next three months?

Overview

1 Do you have any press materials (bio, press release, backgrounder, fact sheets, case studies, data) developed that you can send?

2 If not, please provide a detailed description of who you are and what you do.

3 Can you describe your business in one sentence? If so, what would that be?

4 If you had to pick three key messages you want to always deliver about your business, what would they be?

5 What do you want to be recognized for?

6 What is the story behind your business and/or behind you?

7 What does your business offer in terms of industry trends?

8 What makes your business unique?

9 What are your primary short-term goals?

Target Audience

1 Who is your target audience (gender, age, income, occupation)?

2 What is your target geographic area (local, regional, national, international)?

3 What does your target audience read, watch, and listen to?

4 How does your audience find you?

5 How do you communicate with your audience?

Competition/Peer Group

1 Who are your main competitors?

2 Who do you consider to be #1 in your industry?

3 Are there other thought leaders in your industry who you think have successfully made themselves visible?

4 Why should a media outlet consider you over them?

5 Have you ever opened the newspaper or turned on the news to see/ read a story you felt you should have been a part of?? What was it?

Marketing

1 Have you ever worked with any personalities or celebrities? Do you have any celebrity or other significant endorsements or testimonials?

2 Do you have any existing brand partners? Corporate tie-ins? Cross-promotions? Sponsorships? Endorsements?

3 Do you have any existing partners?

4   Have you ever worked with any organizations (local or national)?

5   What events are you or have you been involved with (trade and consumer)?

Public Relations

1   What are you looking to promote? Your business, yourself, product?

2   Any critical moments coming up that we should know about (launch, funding, new products, etc.)?

3   What media outlets have featured you or your business? Please provide details and links.

4   What are the top 10 media outlets (print, radio, TV, online) you most want to be featured in?

5   What media outlets have you advertised in (if any), and what were the results?

6   Do you contribute (or are you interested in contributing) editorial content to any media channels or websites? If so, what are they? If not, why?

7   Are there any niche websites, blogs, distribution lists, etc., that you regularly read for industry news, or for story ideas?

8   Are analysts something you want us to reach out to, i.e., Forrester?

Personal Brand Building

1   The *Wall Street Journal* and many of the other top tier outlets often publish C-suite focused columns about health regimens, office culture, etc. If you are interested in these opportunities, do you have any unusual routines, office aesthetics, etc., that would be pitch-worthy?

2   Is there anything that doesn't seem linear to PR efforts but that is interesting/noteworthy about you? Anything else like great art or wine collections? Cigars? Cars? Family? Heritage?

Social Media

1   Which social media platform(s) do you currently utilize? Which ones are the most effective?

2   What is the current posting schedule for your website and social channels?

Since this book is focused on earned media, presumably your goals will be around securing these placements. It might be a good to think about reasonable goals for the first quarter and then each subsequent quarter, or to look at the year as a whole. Try to put some measurable KPIs around your goals. For example, a goal can be "Secure one print feature on our company in a national news outlet per quarter."

Once you know what the actual goal is, then you can start developing parameters around how you are going to achieve this goal. One parameter should absolutely be around how many reporters you are reaching out to on a regular basis (whether that be per day, per week or month).

In order to secure press placements, you have to put in time connecting with members of the media. It is very helpful to set a number around that intention. For example, I have a personal goal of sending at least one really perfect, well-thought-out pitch per week to one of my TV contacts. I also have another goal of taking two high-level meetings per month with either a journalist or a potential new client.

Thanks to my growth coach, I have a spreadsheet where I track my progress. Going by week, I reflect each Friday on how I did in each of these areas:

- biggest wins
- biggest failures
- when to double down (on what worked)
- where to develop (on what didn't work)
- feedback received
- upcoming priorities
- self development
- living my values

Develop a system that works for you, but being intentional about your goal-setting and the time and effort you put into these goals will absolutely help you to achieve them.

Who Are We Trying to Reach?

Now that you are aligned on your client's goals, it's important to begin mapping out who you are trying to reach. This involves understanding your core audience or customers and then ascertaining what they read, watch, and listen to. Here are some PR tactics that will likely help you along your journey in earned media relations.

Cision

Cision is a platform that most PR agencies invest in. Cision is earned media software for PR professionals. The platform is a database of every single journalist and media organization *in the world*, that is continually updated and allows users to search for journalists via their physical location and coverage area.

It's usually fairly easy to find a journalist's email address online—oftentimes it's public and right on their profile page of the media outlet; sometimes a journalist includes their email address in their Twitter bio; and if you still can't find it a simple Google search may yield results. However, there are a small number of media professionals whose contact information is not quite as easy to find. This is where Cision comes in and oftentimes it will have that information if you can't find it yourself in a Google search.

The other massive benefit to Cision is that it categorizes journalists by location and coverage area. We'll get into this more in subsequent chapters, but local pitching is a strong strategy when you're trying for your first piece of earned media coverage. The beauty of a platform like Cision is that it saves you *so much time* when you're searching for relevant, local journalists. If you're based in Detroit, Cision can aggregate a list of every single member of the media located in Detroit in about one second. Users can also drill down on topic area and generate a search that will include all Detroit media that cover technology, or health and wellness, or science... you name an industry and you can search for journalists who cover that industry via Cision.

At the time of writing, Cision is not free, and the price depends on the type of access you need. Generally speaking, it will cost at least a few thousand dollars per year for access to the platform. While Cision doesn't actually provide you with too much that you couldn't simply find online with some stealth searches, it does give you back a ton of time in your day when researching journalists.

PR Newswire

PR Newswire, which is part of the same company as Cision, is a distributor of electronic press releases. It's funny to say electronic press releases, because all press releases are electronic today. Many years ago, publicists and agencies printed out press releases and inserted them into folders filled with other press materials that were called "press kits." It's very rare in today's world to see an analog press kit, but sometimes, at events, there may be a table of them for media to take home with them.

Users of PR Newswire (and there are many other similar platforms, too, such as PR Web, Businesswire, etc.—they all essentially offer the same service) are able to upload the press release they've written onto the platform and then select the distribution lists for the release. Distribution lists is a way to say which type of media will be receiving the release (local vs. national; industry coverage area, etc.). The release then gets sent out to assignment desk editors in that distribution release and reporters in that newsroom will get the opportunity to read it. I will note that while putting a release on the wire does not usually yield any earned media placements, it tends to help with search engine optimization (SEO) (more on that in Chapter 9). It also is nice to have a placeholder, so to speak, for the release in a news outlet. It legitimizes the release and gives it the third-party validation of a trusted news source posting it.

It's a common request from clients, or maybe even from your boss, to "put out a press release." Now you know how to do so—you need to call up PR Newswire or another similar type of media company. Again, this service isn't free but various platforms do allow for you to pay per release that you want to distribute, thereby lowering the overall cost versus agencies who have an annual contract with these types of media companies.

Meltwater

Meltwater is a media monitoring company that is used widely amongst those in the PR field. Media monitoring is the activity of monitoring the frequency of print, online, and broadcast media. It can be used in two ways.

The first is to track your clients to see when they are mentioned in the media. Certainly, if you are pitching journalists, in a normal course of action you would know, from the journalist, if and when a story was going to publish that mentions your client. Sometimes, however, for a variety of reasons you may not get that heads-up. Other times still, your company or client may be mentioned in a news story that you didn't even know was about to be published. Meltwater (and there are other similar type of tracking services) provides this for you in real time or with a daily news digest.

The other value it provides is something called "impressions." A media impression is a calculation—it calculates the number of people who have read or watched the piece of earned media coverage you've secured. The value in this is that you have real stats to share with your boss or client, and you can insert these stats into your regular reporting. Similarly, if you are fortunate enough to get your client's story placed in a news aggregate such as the Associated Press or Reuters, it is very likely that *many* other news outlets picked up the story. (This means that they reposted the story on their own website). Sometimes, Google News isn't substantial enough of a search engine to find all of the media placements you're looking for.

HARO

HARO stands for "Help a Reporter Out," and it is also owned by the same good folks at Cision and PR Newswire at the time of this writing. HARO is a digest of reporter requests that gets emailed out to publicists three times per day. It serves as a two-way street:

journalists use it when they need an expert to quote or talk to while reporting a news story. For example, if a reporter is writing about millennials who invest in gold they may send out a request that says they are specifically looking to talk to a millennial who has invested in gold. A reporter may put a request up when he or she is looking for *any* kind of expert—a lawyer, a doctor, a fitness instructor—you name it!

You can sign up for HARO—some options are free, and some are paid. I religiously read each HARO digest three times per day and have found countless great opportunities for my clients through these requests. I have developed relationships with journalists who I first engaged with when replying to their HARO request. It's a great resource for publicists—there may be a perfect request for your client in there!

Agendas and Reporting

Part of your overall goals is going to be to keep your boss, or your client, happy. Clearly, securing earned media coverage is going to be one way to do so. What we have found at Pace PR is that a bi-weekly meeting cadence, where we set forth an agenda that also serves as our reporting system, works very well. Some clients will want to have weekly check-in calls with their agency of record. Some may only want to meet once a month (if everything is going great behind the scenes). Regardless, it's to your benefit to keep everything organized and up to date so that there is always a record of your work. Remember: securing earned media coverage takes time and a lot of hard work—so a report is also a way to showcase all of the time and effort that was put into making those placements happen.

Here is a sample agenda for an update meeting that can serve as a template for you.

CLIENT WEEKLY UPDATE

DATE:

Dial in:

NEW COVERAGE: [*Links to any new coverage since the previous week's call*]

- **Publication:** [*Link*]
- **Publication:** [*Link*]

NEW PRESS OPPS:
[*This is where you put down all new conversations you've had since the last call, the idea being that these move to pending confirmed, but either way they should not stay on the agenda for more than two weeks*]

ONGOING FEEDBACK AND LEADS:
[*Running list of anything that has been confirmed but has not yet run; also can include ongoing conversations that you're still trying to turn into confirmed press, but nothing should stay on the agenda for more than two or three weeks*]

- **Publication:** [*Description of confirmed coverage with expected run date*]
- **Publication:** [*Description of confirmed coverage with expected run date*]

PITCHING STRATEGY:
[*List of any and all active pitches you're working on for that week; plans for new pitch angles to be drafted or scheduled for outreach the following week*]

ADDITIONAL OPPORTUNITIES FOR DISCUSSION:
[*List of other activities you are working on for the client. This can include events, op-ed drafting, research, strategic introductions, conferences, etc.*]

ALL PRESS COVERAGE TO DATE:
[*Link to list of press coverage secured on behalf of the client*]

OPTIONAL:

- Goals:
- Total impressions to date:

Social Media

This may sound so basic, but to achieve your goal of earned media placements you need to spend a certain amount of time on social media every day. Journalists *live* on social media, particularly Twitter and Instagram, so start following the most relevant journalists to you so you can see what they're posting about. Sometimes they may post in need of a source (win!). Sometimes they may opine on an issue. Sometimes they may share a recent article they wrote. Regardless, if media relations are your goal then you have to start keeping up with the media that will help you achieve those goals.

If appropriate, comment or re-share what they've posted. It's important to try to have a more genuine and authentic connection on social media for it to actually yield any results. But the other benefit of being active on social media is that then the journalist will not only recognize your name from receiving your pitches to his or her inbox, but they'll also start seeing you pop up on social. You want to become a known quantity to these journalists, and being active on social is one way to help you achieve that goal.

The Importance of Goals

In the world of public relations, one lesson stands out above the rest: the importance of setting clear goals. Without clearly defined goals, you can wind up spinning your wheels and working very hard without achieving the results you're looking for. Setting goals is important in all aspects of life, including running a business, executing client work, and pursuing personal and professional growth. Without a sense of direction, all our efforts are for naught.

So, what are your goals? Have you taken the time to reflect on this question? It's high time you did. Start by examining your job description. Ideally, the objectives for your role in publicizing your brand or company should be clearly outlined. But if they are not, it's time to take charge of your career and establish these goals for yourself. You may need to be an advocate for yourself and your position within the company to achieve this, but it will be worth it.

As a PR professional, your overarching goal is likely to secure earned media coverage for your company, brand, or CEO/founder. But why? What is the purpose behind this objective? To gain clarity, you must ask yourself and your team why PR is necessary, what you hope to achieve, and who your target audience is. These inquiries will help you better understand your goals, allowing you to develop strategies that align with your overall objectives.

So, having a clear sense of direction is crucial to the success of any PR campaign. Take the time to establish your objectives and discuss them with your team to ensure everyone is working towards the same destination. By doing so, you can create targeted strategies that drive results and ultimately help you achieve your desired outcomes. Remember, in PR, knowing where you're headed is everything, so set your sights on success before you take that first step.

The Brand's Elevator Pitch

05

A critical step to take *prior* to pursuing earned media opportunities is to first create your brand's elevator pitch.

An elevator pitch is how someone explains themselves, or their company, in about 30 seconds. It's called an *elevator* pitch because, as legend has it, you're supposed to be able to "pitch" yourself to whomever you're stuck in an elevator with—for the length of that ride (very short, usually!). This is a phenomenal exercise to implement as it will truly help you not only when you're speaking with the media but also when you're talking to clients, customers, investors, colleagues, and other stakeholders.

So, how do you create an elevator pitch? As mentioned, an elevator pitch can be for you, personally, which helps a ton if/when you're looking to change careers, find a new job or get a promotion. For the purpose of this chapter, let's start with the elevator pitch for the brand, i.e., for your company.

To begin, ask yourself the following questions:

- What does my company do?
- Why do clients or customers want to work with us?
- What do we do that is better or different than anyone else?
- What makes us stand out?
- When someone asks me what I do and what my company does, what is my standard response?

Write all of your answers down. Then, ask your manager, boss, and colleagues if they would participate in this exercise as well. If you're the head of PR or comms for your organization, it doesn't necessarily mean that you should, solely, be developing your brand's elevator pitch without input from others on the team.

Once you have as many responses from internal colleagues as possible, think about if you have friendly customers, clients, or former customers/clients whom you can approach with these same set of questions. This should only be done with those you feel very comfortable with—you don't want to arouse any suspicion or make this awkward with a client—but oftentimes, the want that a *client* describes can hold a ton of valuable intel. After all, they are the ones paying the company for its services, and hopefully they are referring you business as well. If you have any doubts, ask your manager if he or she thinks this is appropriate.

Next, you'll want to conduct some competitive analysis and research. The way to start is to identify the three to five top competitors in your space and research them as much as possible. A lot of this research can be done quite simply over the internet.

First, go to their websites and carefully review the language they use to describe the company. A brand's elevator pitch is not going to be spelled out, written word-for-word on their website... but they may have a useful tag-line right there on the home page that could spark some ideas for this exercise. Make sure to visit their "About" section—obviously this section has information that describes their practice and could spark ideas for your own elevator pitch. Lastly, check to see if they have client testimonials anywhere—hearing straight from clients as to why they found the partnership valuable will provide you with a ton of context as you're developing the brand's elevator pitch.

You want to make sure you also visit their social media handles—even though a company's website and *all* of its corresponding social media should be uniform in its messaging. You'd be surprised how many are not. Look for the same prompts in their messaging. Again, this may inform you with some ideas as you begin to develop your own elevator pitch.

Now that you have input from several of your co-workers and have conducted research on competitors, it's time to start writing your company's brand elevator pitch. An elevator pitch can be as short as three sentences but should be no longer than two paragraphs. The first words should be your company name and describe as simply as you can what you do. I'll use the first sentence of my company as an example:

> Pace Public Relations is a PR agency specializing in media relations—which means, we get our clients featured in the media.

Describe what your company does... but if your industry or company is a bit nuanced or complicated, it's OK to add in another explainer like I did above. Typically, when I find myself in a situation where I'm giving my company's elevator pitch, it's *not* to others in the PR industry. Usually, it's when I'm in the company of founders or CEOs who either have no, or little, understanding of the PR world. Some many even have a negative connotation of the PR industry—perhaps they've been burned working with an agency in the past. I don't want to assume that they automatically know the term "media relations," which is why I spell it out.

In the next sentence, go even further to describe more granularly how you do what you do and why the person on the receiving end should care. Start by piquing their interest. We can continue here with my example:

> We work with national television producers, top podcasts and reporters
> at major newspapers and websites to help get our clients featured
> in them. The result is that our clients universally see a benefit to
> their business—mostly through an increase in brand awareness and
> credibility and legitimacy.

As you can see here, I get pretty specific. I mention national TV producers and the other types of media we work with. I make it painfully obvious that our clients, as a result of our work, get featured in those media outlets—and then I go on to specify exactly how those clients benefit from our work—through the increase in their own brand awareness and credibility and legitimacy. By positioning the work we do in the context of current clients, I'm simply informing the person I'm pitching about our work—I'm not being salesy (yet).

The final part of your elevator pitch can, and likely should, be more overt, and close with one line about how you'd like to work together. My final line is usually something like this:

If you think your company could benefit from media exposure—maybe even you could see yourself on TV discussing the work you do—then we should talk about the potential ways we can work together.

In this instance, the work I'm doing for clients requires the CEO to be the media representative for the company and go on TV and conduct interviews. It's a nuance that, for me, is handled carefully as not every CEO *wants* to be seen on TV, and furthermore, sometimes the person I'm talking to doesn't even *want* PR for their company—some larger corporations actually pay people to keep them *out* of the news. My point in telling you this is that, once you have written down a brand elevator pitch that you're proud of, remember that it can and should be adapted and slightly changed based on who you're talking to and your knowledge of their needs. Delivering a great elevator pitch requires a high level of EQ. My best piece of advice, as it pertains to the EQ portion of an elevator pitch, is to *listen* first. You'll learn a lot by just listening; and most people will fill in awkward silences by blabbing on about themselves. Listen. Listen intently. Nod your head and try to really hear what they're saying. You may get clues or little prompts that will help you to identify what exactly you have to offer that could be interesting to them.

Now it's time to think about the delivery of your elevator pitch. You should assume that the first time you find yourself delivering your company's elevator pitch you will be totally frazzled, caught off guard and not prepared. That's because you probably won't even recognize you're *delivering* your elevator pitch until you're right in the middle of it. It's not like you can set up a meeting and say to a prospective client, "Let's schedule a meeting so I can share my elevator pitch with you." You can certainly schedule a prospective new business meeting—or at least conduct the outreach to *try* to secure that meeting—but that will likely include various members of your team, a presentation, and that the person or persons on the receiving end of the meeting will have already googled you and done their own research. An elevator pitch is in the moment—off the cuff—spur of the moment. So, beyond having the words written down, it's critically important that you practice your delivery as well.

In the class I teach on PR consulting at NYU's Graduate School of Professional Studies, I ask each of my students to stand up and deliver their personal elevator pitch. While many of them have begun their professional journey with entry-level jobs in the field, they are mostly still young and green and haven't done a ton of public speaking. This exercise (which isn't graded!) tends to evoke fear in most or all of them... which actually is a good thing.

Many people have a fear of public speaking, especially if they're speaking on a topic they don't feel confident about. Presuming you've never had a PR-specific elevator pitch prior to reading this book, then you would never have spoken the pitch aloud. That may induce some fear in you. Nothing can squash fear like practicing.

Practice your elevator pitch! Practice it in the mirror. Practice it on your roommates, your family, your friends. Call a meeting at your company where you all practice out loud to each other your own unique versions of the pitch. Support each other for doing a great job and offer constructive feedback when necessary. Remember that an elevator pitch is much more successful if the person delivering it is confident. Confidence comes much more naturally if you have good posture and stand up straight. Looking someone in the eye automatically makes them trust you more... but, as humans, we are less likely to make eye contact when speaking (but more likely to maintain eye contact when listening to someone else).

Doing PR means putting your corporation, or your clients, "out there." But a lot of PR is putting *yourself* out there, too. Having your own elevator pitch is something each and every one of you should also have perfected—but, chances are, you have not even thought about a personalized elevator pitch for yourself—until now.

Having your own elevator pitch can help your company get media placements. Producers and reporters only want to work with smart, reliable publicists, who make their job seamless. You can, and should, create an elevator pitch that you can call upon when you are in the first, early conversations with members of the media. It can go something like this:

A big part of my job is securing media placements for my company. I love working with journalists to make their lives easier and getting them the best and most relevant information as quickly as possible. I'm proud of my work and the fact that I have real relationships in the media.

This will signal to the reporter that you're someone to be trusted. They will then know that you understand how the process works and some of the areas that are important as they work on the story.

As you progress in your career, you may find that your personal elevator pitch and the company's morph together. You may find it difficult sometimes to discern between the two—or maybe even struggle to know when to use which one. It's a good problem to have—it means that the brand you're working for is wrapped up your own good work and that the two are inextricably linked.

I discussed this very thing on a recent podcast, the Smart Agency Masterclass. I'm providing a (lightly edited) transcript here so you can start to think more deeply about your own personal brand and elevator pitch in the context of the corporation you work for. Enjoy!

EXPERT INSIGHT

Jason: What's up, agency owners! Jason Swank here, and I have another amazing guest. We're going to talk about how she's grown her agency. There's always been this debate, if you should build your personal brand or focus more on branding your agency. Today we're going to talk about that and how they built multiple offices all over the world. So, let's go ahead and get into the show. Hey Annie, welcome to the show.

Annie: Hi. Thanks for having me.

Jason: So, tell us who you are and what you do.

Annie: Sure. So, my name is Annie Pace Scranton and I run a PR agency called Pace Public Relations. We are based in New York, but we have offices and clients around the country and globally. And we primarily focus on helping our clients get great media attention and media placements, so that way they can highlight the good work that they're doing.

Jason: Awesome. And tell us, how did you get started in creating an agency?

Annie: It all started when I lost my job at CNBC. I was a producer there and the show I was working on got canceled. I found myself at the age of 28 without a job, without much savings. So, I did what any young girl would do. I called my mom, crying, and said, "What am I going to do now?" And then I really pulled myself together and sent an email out to everyone in my network saying, "I need a job. Let me know if you hear of anything." And a publicist who I had worked with frequently booking his clients on CNBC said to me, "I don't think you've had any formal PR training, but if you can help me get media for my current client, I'll pay you." And it came very naturally and easy to me. I texted my friend in the newsroom and she responded, "Oh, this guy looks great. Can he come on the show tomorrow?" And that was kind of my "light bulb" moment where I realized my "special currency" was that I had worked at many different news outlets and knew a lot of really influential and important producers and reporters, and would be able to help brands, companies, CEOs, and founders get that access to the media that they were wanting to have.

Jason: So, the important question is, how much did you charge them, or how much did you get paid for the first gig?

Annie: Oh, not very much at all. Honestly, I feel like I undercharged for many, many years, way longer than I should have. I think it's probably a common issue that start-ups and founders have. At the time I had accepted a full-time job at another news network, so I was doing this on the side, so it wasn't quite as important to make exactly as much money as I needed to, since I had that cushion and security. But it quickly it morphed into a monthly retainer model, which is what most PR agencies do. When I first started out, I think I charged a thousand bucks a month, and now our retainers normally are around $10,000 a month. But I'm 12 years in business, so, you know, that's kind of been the trajectory of our growth.

Jason: How long did it take you from doing this on the side to saying, "All right, I'm quitting this other position and I'm going to do this full time." And then what were the steps that you took?

Annie: It took about a year and a half. When I was making equal amounts of money from doing it on the side as I was for my full-time job I realized, "You know what, it's now or never. I'm 30 years old. I do have a little bit of a safety net and a little bit of money in the bank. Let me just take a risk." I resigned, and crowdsourced everybody I knew. I was fortunate because working in TV news and booking guests introduced me to a ton of people. I called up an attorney I was close with, and I said, "If I'm going to do this full time what do I do?" And he said, "You need to incorporate." And I said, "What does that mean?"

He asked me a bunch of questions and said, "You should be an S corp. I'll file it for you." I paid him and he did it. Then I found a web designer who put together a very basic website for me. I stopped using my Gmail and got an app that pays public relations email addresses. PR is a service industry, so there's not actually a ton of steps that you need to put in place before you start. I wasn't manufacturing a product; I didn't have to answer to investors or anything like that. All I needed was my laptop, my phone and Wi-Fi. I did learn the hard way about finding a good accountant, because I didn't really realize how much money I was going to need to put aside for taxes. I had always been a W2 employee, and that money had always been taken out of my paycheck for me. A big piece of advice I have for people who are starting out on their own is get a good accountant and put aside as much money as you can. Because it's a rough reality when that first tax bill comes.

Jason: What about when you started hiring people? I find, especially with many agency owners that start by accident, like you did, they say, "All right, everything is me, so now I need to kind of step it up." How? Who did you hire? Not particularly a name, but what position, and then how did you start training them to do the things that you were doing?

Annie: I realized I needed my first employee when I just had way too much work to handle. I realized I was doing more low-level admin things and it was taking up so much of my time. I realized my time should be spent getting new business, and working on fine-tuning my relationships with the media—the key things that only I could do given the position that I was in. So, I found somebody who had a background in media who was looking. I was at a party talking to a mutual friend and was introduced to this guy and just vibed with him. I liked him right away.

I trained him by working side-by-side with him in a very small office. We talked through every single thing that was going on. He was a quick learner. He was very responsible, and it was one of the best decisions I ever made, because, now I had to put someone on payroll, I had to make sure that I had enough money to pay them. I said, "You know what, if I don't try it, what's the alternative? I can't work literally 24 hours a day." I think every business owner gets to that point. It can be a good decision. You just have to have the confidence in yourself that you can do it.

Jason: There's always a debate that I see in my mastermind groups or agency owners that we chat with. And this is what I did at our agency early on. I put all my personal effort into marketing the agency and none into marketing myself or creating any content. So, what, what are your feelings around that?

Annie: I think that you need to do both. For the type of agency that I have and what I can speak to is that 75 percent of it is wrapped up in me because I started it, and for so long it was just me and one or two staff members. So, when people think of Annie Scranton, it's synonymous with public relations because of how entrenched my work is in my day-to-day life. But I think now more than ever consumers want to work with companies or brands that they believe in, and they can attach to a specific person. Not just, "Oh, I love Nike, so let me follow Nike on social media." It's "What are your favorite athletes or celebrities that are wearing those brands?"

People want to follow founders because they are aspirational. You want to see them succeed. You want to see their journey and their career path. So, I think doing the branding for yourself as an agency owner or C-suite executive is extremely important. I think it reels people in, in a way that's different when you're only promoting a brand, because it's not as personal.

Jason: I agree with that. Now, since you're doing so much personal branding, when a client comes to your agency are you doing everything for them?

Annie: No.

Jason: That's what everybody thinks when they start branding themselves. They literally think, "Well, if I brand myself, my agency's not worth anything and then I have to do everything." Because when someone comes in, they want you.

Annie: True. But to a much lesser degree now. I mean, I'm 12 years in, and so I'm in a very different place than when I was working out of my studio apartment when I was 28 years old. But if you're going to start an agency or any business for the first few years, you're going to be doing most of it yourself and you have to be okay with that. And perhaps you're going to be one of those people that can scale up super, super fast, but it may take longer. So if you don't love what you're doing and you don't want to do the work, then I would suggest doing something else in your career. But I think there is absolutely a path forward. If you hire really good, smart people to work with you, and you train them well, then you don't have to do everything yourself and you shouldn't have to. I think it's such a misconception that everybody needs to evolve in their career and get to a place where they're growing and learning new things and doing different things. That's the way that you provide value to your clients and to your agency.

Jason: What are some examples of building your personal brand that have worked really well for you?

Annie: I spend a lot of time posting and interacting on LinkedIn, and I can't speak enough about that platform. I have gotten tons of new business leads from LinkedIn. Talking about personal branding, it's not just saying, "I got this new client" or "Check out this awesome thing about my business." It's actually talking about a news story that's happening. I'll write a short post where I position myself as a subject matter expert or thought leader, as it relates to the news. I believe that's a way that you can be consistent about continually putting your personal branding and your messaging out there. I also have had the fortune of doing different webinars or seminars or speaking engagements where I talk about personal branding. I talk about it a lot with our clients. One of the first things I'll probably ask them is, "How do you describe yourself? I'm going to set you up with a producer or reporter— how do you tell them who you are in 30 seconds?" I try to live that out in my day-to-day life by all forms of communication, whether it's with a client or prospective client or just people who are in the same industry as myself

Jason: On positioning, I feel that's really important for the elevator pitch. Rather than saying always get so frustrated when I look at someone's LinkedIn profile or someone talks to me and they just go, "I'm an agency owner." I'm like, "What does that mean?" Like it doesn't mean anything. What is ...

Annie: The agency? It's all me. [*Laugh*]

Jason: Yeah, exactly. So, what is the best way to position your personal brand in those 20 seconds that you have?

Annie: First of all, if it takes you longer than 20 seconds to describe who you are and what you do, you need to sit down and figure out what your elevator pitch is, what your personal brand is, and how you can say that concisely. Something that I found really valuable is, you have to always think about what is in it for the person you're talking to and listening to. People are busy, we have a million and one distractions, we have no attention span anymore. Nobody wants to hear you drone on and on about what you do, but if you can say to them, "Here's what I do and here's how it can help you,"—okay, well now you've got my attention a little bit. Okay, you can help my business grow, you can help me get new clients, you can make my workflow processes easier, whatever. Always think about what's the ROI for the other person. And I think that that will help your messaging immensely.

Jason: What's the worst pitch you've ever heard?

Annie: Well, when I was producing, I worked at HLN, which is CNN's sister network. I worked for an anchor named Jane Villa Mitchell. If you watched her show, it was a nightly show. She was on before Nancy Grace. So, we called her "Nancy Grace light." She always talked about crime, and missing girls, that kind of thing. It was a heavy crime news show. I know Jane and if you looked her up for one second on the internet, you would know that she is three things: a vegan, a recovering alcoholic, and a lesbian. And that's Jane. I got a pitch in my inbox from somebody who said, "Hey Annie, I'm working with this new tequila company, and we would love to come on and do a live taste test with Jane on the air and she could try the different tequilas and blah, blah, blah."

And I just wrote this person back and I was like, "This pitch is wrong on so many levels. We're a new show, we focus on crime, and Jane has been sober for 30 years." So they apologized and said, "I'm so sorry. You were on a big email blast that we did, and we didn't mean for it to come in your inbox." But that totally discredited that person to me and put her on my "Do not ever interact with" file. When you're pitching, know who you're pitching to, take five minutes to research, and that can go a long way.

Jason: They should have sent you guys a steak as an apology.

Annie: Then she would've really been off!

Jason: Yeah, it's unbelievable how many times people don't research ahead of time, and it drives me absolutely nuts.

Annie: There's just no excuse. Now there's this thing called the internet, everybody's on social media. Even the media reporters are people too. They have Instagram accounts, they're on LinkedIn, they're on Twitter. It's not just researching, it's also gathering information and then being informed because it will help you put together an email that will be so much more effective. It doesn't always also need to be transactional, "I'm emailing you so I can get X." Think about just reaching out to people in the spirit of collaboration, developing a relationship and telling somebody, "I really enjoyed reading your last few pieces," that's going to go a long way. Then when there is a moment where you have a pitch that you want to get in front of them with, hopefully they'll remember because you've been in touch with them before in a genuine way.

Jason: Last question, I'm curious about as, as we're recording this in—what, March 2022? I can't even remember anymore! It just seems like everything blurred when, you know, the virus came out, but a lot of people I've seen started saying, "You have offices all over. Why not be virtual?" I always love to hear everybody's thoughts on that.

Annie: Media is all over that, and that's what we focus on. So, I think having a footprint in key cities is advantageous for that reason. We were virtual for the better part of these past two years, for obvious reasons. But PR is a collaborative and creative industry and there are ideas and moments sparked when you're in an office together or at the proverbial water cooler that cannot be replicated over Zoom or in a virtual setting. We could work virtually for forever, but I don't want that. I've developed some of my best relationships and friendships from being in-person and going with a client to an interview or attending a media event or going to this networking conference or whatever. It helps you learn and remember how to interact with people. We already don't know how to talk to each other. So, if we were virtual all the time, you would lose a lot of that. And my job is to communicate all day long. So that's why.

Jason: Yeah, I always love to see so many people getting rid of their offices and going virtual, but I totally agree with you. I remember when I ran Solar Velocity, there's so many invaluable moments in the office, whether it be the office pranks that we would pull (they hung my desk from the ceiling once and gave me a little school desk. I'm a big guy, I do not fit in a school desk)—it's all those little things that you miss that make that culture much better.

Annie: In this moment in time when it's really hard to hire and retain talent, part of what people makes people happy about their job is the work that they're doing, but it's also the people, and you lose that when you're only talking to someone on Slack or Zoom all day long. I think that's another component to it as well.

Jason: Awesome. Well, Annie, this has all been amazing. Thanks so much for coming on the show!

Before pursuing earned media opportunities, a well-crafted elevator pitch must be devised to communicate your brand's unique selling proposition effectively. In addition to being essential for media pitches, it can also serve as a tool for communicating with clients, investors, and colleagues. Creating an elevator pitch requires thoughtful consideration of your company's purpose, its differentiating factors, and the value it brings to its clients. This exercise can be done individually, but getting input from others in the organization, including managers, bosses, and colleagues, is beneficial. Collaboration will allow for diverse perspectives, resulting in a well-rounded and compelling pitch that captures the essence of your brand.

This is not a one-time exercise; it should be reviewed and revised regularly to reflect changes in the company's goals, services, or target audience. The elevator pitch serves as a foundation for building your brand's messaging, making it an essential element of your company's branding strategy.

In essence, a well-crafted elevator pitch can be the difference between successfully communicating your brand's value and failing to capture the attention of potential clients, investors, or the media. Take the time to create an effective pitch, collaborate with others in your organization, and continue to refine it as your company grows and evolves.

Thought Leadership

06

"Thought leadership" is a term you've likely heard tossed around… but maybe you don't actually know what it means or how to apply it to your day-to-day work. In its simplest form, thought leadership encompasses the process of building up the public profile of one or more leaders. When I say "public" profile, I don't necessarily singularly mean media-facing, but certainly, that's a part of it. Thought leadership is one area that any PR professional who is dedicated to her or his craft can easily refine and apply to their daily comms work—depending, of course, on how easily you can access the thought leaders within your company.

So, what is a thought leader? According to Business News Daily, a thought leader "is someone who, based on their expertise and perspective in an industry, offers unique guidance, inspires innovation, and influences others."[1] In reality, *anyone* can be a thought leader. Truly. Even you, the wonderful individual reading this book, are—or can become—a thought leader.

For the purposes of this chapter, we need to focus our thinking about thought leadership and the corresponding thought leaders on your clients and C-suite executives. Think of the leadership team within your company or within your client's organization—the founder, the CEO, the president and anyone else in the C-suite. Those folks are, generally speaking, the most commonly sought-after thought leaders that PR professionals work with. The founder or CEO's public profile can also mean the profile, or rather, image, that he or she presents to the employees at the company, to investors, to customers, to key stakeholders, and yes, of course, to the public.

The simplest way to think of thought leadership is as follows: to have your client present their thoughts, in some public manner, on relevant trends, insights, or news within your industry. Having trouble figuring out how to do that for your client or CEO? Here's an example. Let's say you run comms at an electric battery company, and Tesla's stock plummets suddenly. Your CEO may have some insights as to why that is happening. Or, let's say, new data comes out that says Americans are buying more electric vehicles (EVs) than ever before. Certainly, your CEO *should* have something to say about that.

A critical step towards being successful in the field of thought leadership is to first determine what your client, and the brand behind the client, is best suited to speak on. It's hard to *teach* this, but a good way to start is by first simply determining which industry your client is in. Is it tech? Fitness? Healthcare?

Once you determine the larger industry, get more granular. Within the tech industry, is it software-as-a-service (SaaS)? Property technology? Within fitness, is it fitness technology? A new product launch? Within healthcare, is it pharma? Health administration?

It sounds basic, but make sure you *really* understand the larger industry, and then the sub-industry, your company is in. One tactic for this work might be to do your own online research on the company—see what articles have already been published. Read carefully the text on your website. Ask those questions of colleagues or your manager.

The reason for this always reverts back to the *goals* of the company. You can conduct the greatest thought leadership campaign in the history of all thought leadership campaigns—but if the end results don't revert back to the goals of the company, then it's for naught. Part of this work will likely bring you on an introspective journey into the company, its founders, and its leaders. Let me explain.

While having your thought leaders opine on industry news is one very clear and excellent form of thought leadership, you also want to understand your thought leaders' unique experiences and, thus, the unique value that they bring to the company and to the industry. This may be a delicate process, since it's going to require you to *really* get to know those thought leaders in a more personal way. But the end result can, and should, be content that highlights the inherent significance of them within the industry.

The Most Common Types of Thought Leaders

Founder

Let's start with the founder. If you're lucky enough to work with the founder of your organization, chances are he or she has a fairly compelling origin story of how they created the company. You want to tap into that and find out very specifically about their background before they became a founder. What lessons did they learn along the way? Was there a light bulb moment that gave them the idea for the business? What was their biggest triumph? Their biggest failure? What's their philosophy on leadership? What do they think makes a great leader? Why do some founders succeed and others fail?

All of these questions and subsequent answers will give you a *ton* to work with as you build out a thought leadership campaign.

As a starting point, make sure you are prepared. First, start by conducting an exhaustive Google search of the founder. There's a high likelihood that the internet will provide you with a lot of the information you're looking for. Next, approach some of the C-suite executives who perhaps know the founder really well and ask them for any key moments that were exceptionally inspiring. A great way to get a glimpse into the personality of the founder is to interview those who were hired directly by them—this may reveal traits and characteristics that exemplify their leadership. And, then, you also have a great personal story to add to future promotional materials.

Next, if you are lucky enough to have face time with the founder, write down your questions in advance so that you can control the conversation. Since you've already done the prep work ahead of this interview, now is the time to make sure your questions are very personalized ("I know that when you lost that one big deal, it really caused you to re-evaluate the focus of the company") as opposed to generic ("Was there a watershed moment that changed the course of the company?").

If you can, try to get to the heart of *why* they created the company; what problem were they looking to solve; what their greater purpose and mission evolved into; and then… where to, from here? In PR you should *always* be thinking about how to advance the story and the narrative in support of your leaders.

Lastly, make sure are mindful of their time and do not take longer than 45 minutes. Be sure to send a thank you note after. And certainly, make sure you understand the approvals process for pitching the founder. Understand what he or she is willing to do *before* you approach the media or put anything out that is public-facing.

CEO

The CEO thought leadership track is going to be more closely related to the success of the company, which will also tie into the greater industry. Getting her or his background details are less important— understanding exactly how the current business model fits into the needs of the industry is where the real value of this exercise lies.

You may want to consider asking your CEO about the company's growth in recent years. How have they expanded and evolved as a brand? What needs did the industry have that the company was able to answer? What were the moments that precipitated growth or evolution of the business?

You're going to also want to ask, in as much detail as possible, what makes your organization different? Why would someone—a customer, a client, an investor—choose to align with your company over any other? Finding the answers to these questions will help you immensely as you begin the thought leadership process.

Other Examples of Thought Leaders

While the founder and CEO are the two most common types of thought leaders, your organization may have other C-suite executives that would be important in your promotional efforts. Examples include any other manager within your organization, but most common are:

Chief Marketing Officer

There are several trade publications and mainstream reporters dedicated to covering the field of marketing—so it could be an easy "win" as you take your thought leadership to press.

Female or Diverse Leaders

If you are able to work with, and highlight, diverse leaders within your organization it will open up your outreach efforts. These leaders will undoubtedly have unique experiences that, once understood and laid out, will likely not only present your company in a positive light, but also provide others with key insights and takeaways to help them on their own professional journey.

Young Leaders

There are many media outlets dedicated to younger working professionals, so tap into any rising stars within your organization. Remember that thought leadership tactics often have more than one benefit—by highlighting some of your younger team members, it may wind up aiding in recruiting efforts.

In summary, thought leadership is a way to put your company's leaders "out there" to gain exposure. But the best part of thought leadership is that it's inherently not salesy. The entire point of thought leadership is to *not* promote, in an overt way, your company or your initiatives. The point is to take your leaders' collective years of experience and apply that in a meaningful way to relevant industry news.

So, how do you do that? There are several ways to engage in thought leadership tactics. The most common is via the written word, which we'll break down below into owned media tactics and then earned media. We'll also discuss podcasting and video efforts. The key here is to put the main takeaways from your thought leaders into a finished product that is effective and will be positioned to both benefit the brand and provide key insights for the reader, listener, or viewer at home.

Owned Media[2]

Owned media is just that—"media" that your company or organization owns itself. If you're creating content for owned media, it means that you are in control. You don't have to think about external parameters like you would with a media organization. You have free reign. Except now... you have to actually *write* the content.

The process of figuring out drafting content for clients is a tricky one. Do not get discouraged if this process takes on several different iterations over the course of your career. Writing is personal—and sometimes it takes a few shots before your thought leader really connects with a writer who "gets" them.

So first: is there a writer on your team? If not, is there someone who is a good writer who could potentially take this role on? If not, does your team have budget to hire an external writer? If not... then you may be the new writer of all owned media!

I kid, I kid. For many thought leaders, they actually *prefer* to write their own content, for the reasons I just mentioned. Sometimes it's just easier to write something that sounds like you if you're the one actually writing it. If this is the case, then you'll just need to have a critical eye in the editing process, making sure that the writer's goals and missions are clear within a purpose-driven piece of content. That's not easy but if you prep them *ahead of time*, it's much more attainable.

The first step is to figure out what, exactly, the headline of the piece will be. Make sure it is purpose-driven—meaning, it's going to be a piece that readers will benefit and learn from. You might even want to write out the purpose and mission of the greater thought leadership campaign on a post-it note for your thought leader. Or share a Google Doc of the piece with the purpose and mission in the comments section—that way, the writer will remember to always keep it in mind.

And just what is the purpose of this thought leadership campaign? For each reader of this book it will, of course, be different. However, for all, you'll want to make the time to explain to your thought leaders that the overall goal is to make their name and brand synonymous with innovative, forward-focused products and services.

If your thought leader actually wants you to write the entire piece, from soup to nuts, then you're going to need to have a fairly extensive pre-interview process in which you absolutely record the conversation and have it transcribed. Oftentimes, it helps to come into that conversation with several suggested headlines and perhaps even a central thesis of what the piece will be. This will help you to ask the most direct questions possible to get the answers you need. Oftentimes, a follow-up conversation may be necessary with several rounds of edits. You likely will not have time to take this on yourself, in addition to all of your other responsibilities. But, if you have to, hopefully this information will provide some guideposts as you begin the process.

Website

Each website should have a "News" section. News doesn't have to mean the 6 o'clock local news you turn on or the paper you read in the morning. News can also be owned, and you're ready to start creating written content in cooperation with your thought leaders. There are several types of owned media you can put in the news section of your company's website.

Announcements

Anytime there is a new hire, a big event, a new partnership, or company news, this can be a moment for you to "create" news in the form of owned media. Certainly, you should be writing a corresponding press release to commemorate these moments and have a formal record of their happening. But you could also ask your various thought leaders to write a short (100 words, even) piece on their perspective on the news. Include a picture and then you have the formal release, a photo, and a little write-up. That's easy to share on social media and will make all parties happy.

Industry-Related Commentary

Generally speaking, on a company's website, you're going to want to keep the content within the news section to industry-related pieces. If you're having trouble figuring out *what* exactly your thought leader should write about, start by reading your industry's trade publications and see if that sparks any ideas. You should also set up Google Alerts for relevant keywords within your industry to see if that generates a topic. But what would likely work the easiest and be most streamlined is if you could do the aforementioned and then get a meeting with your thought leader to discuss, so you can hear her or his own personal take on the issue.

For the website, these pieces can be around 500 words or so—they do not have to be, and should not be, very lengthy. While they should center around industry news, since this is owned media this is a completely appropriate time to layer in ways in which your company fits into the conversation.

Media Mentions

Anytime you get a press mention, you will now start to make sure your web team posts it under the news section of the website. But, what's even better than just posting the link with the title is if the C-suite member who was interviewed could write a very short post about the experience. This will help with SEO purposes but also will make the post more engaging—and much easier to share on social media.

Social Media

Thought leadership absolutely has developed into social media content creation, meaning, whatever pieces you've written, recorded or shot can—and likely should—be promoted on social media accordingly. All of this is done with the aim of building the brand awareness for your thought leader and driving home the goal and mission of the company.

So, how do you maximize thought leadership on social media? Let's break it down by the most-utilized social platforms—but it's very important first to have a conversation with the C-suite about how public facing they want their leaders to be on social media. Some companies, as a rule, do not want their employees to be active whatsoever on social media. Full stop. Some organizations are OK with it, but to an extent (i.e., don't put your political leanings out there). And then, some are fine with their employees letting loose with no rules at all on social. For the majority of companies, it will be somewhere in the middle. But you're just going to want to make sure you understand the protocol in place from this point moving forward—and to understand, or even potentially create, an approval process for tweets going out under specific employee handles.

Twitter

Twitter is a social media platform that only works if you really work it. What I mean is, you need to be a frequent tweeter, otherwise it will be very challenging to gain followers and traction. You can advise your thought leaders that if they don't have time to write an entire piece, taking their thoughts to Twitter *may* be a useful exercise in increasing their thought leadership. At a minimum, it could be a good forum to get your thought leaders in the habit of *thinking* of themselves as thought leaders.

LinkedIn

LinkedIn is likely the most common, and effective, social media platform when it comes to thought leadership. LinkedIn is a platform that celebrates the humble (or not so humble) brag when it comes to one's job and career. *Anytime* there is a "win" for your thought leader—e.g., a new client signed on, a new hire was made, a partnership was formed, numbers were released—these could all potentially be a relevant post for thought leadership. It's important, though, to walk your client through some ins and outs of how to most effectively post on LinkedIn.

Let's take the example of a new hire made within the company. Your CEO would like to take that opportunity to write a short, thought-leadership driven post celebrating the news.

Here is an example of an ineffective post:

Today we announced the hire of our new Account Manager, Jane Smith. Jane's experience is sure to help our teams to communicate more effectively. Welcome, Jane!

That post essentially tells me nothing—and honestly, is a "waste" of a post. What I mean by waste is that you can post too much on social media. If you do, people will start to ignore it or float over your posts. You do need to be choosy when it comes to what and how you're posting.

Let's write a sample post that would be more effective. Remember to always revert back to the goals of the company and the goals of your thought leader. Let's say the goal of the company is to break into a new industry for sales and your thought leader's goal is to move from managing staff to focusing time on bigger picture projects. If that's the case, here is one example of how that post could be written:

> At [company name], we have enjoyed and flourished working in the aerospace and healthcare industries since the company was founded 10 years ago. Today marks a special moment for us—as we bring on JANE DOE, Account Manager, to our team. Jane comes from a long and storied sales career, primarily in the defense space. Jane will be spearheading, under my supervision, a new sales category for private defense contractors. We are all thrilled to see the great work we know Jane will do. For me, personally, this hire means a lot as I'll be working with Jane in the coming months to continue our expansion into other verticals. Stay tuned for more exciting news from us in the months to come!

When you're posting on LinkedIn, remember that prospective employees, investors, and clients/customers are continually reading and watching what you're posting. So you want to, of course, put your best foot forward in the post but you should also craft your post by design—so you can attract the types of viewers you're looking for. Being as specific as possible will help with that.

Newsletters

If your company doesn't currently have a newsletter, or an e-newsletter (much more common and sensible), this may be an area that you want to develop and "own" in the months or year ahead.

The purpose of a newsletter is to compile all of your biggest "wins" and news over the past year or quarter (typically, newsletters, while they *can* go out once per week, go out once per quarter, twice a year or annually) condensed into one easy-to-read format. It's a way to, in one email, *know* that the email is getting into the inbox of hundreds, potentially thousands, of related contacts to your business.

E-newsletters are most commonly curated via a template such as Mailchimp. I would recommend this as a place to start, since you can easily choose your own template, which also allows you to add in photos, making your newsletter more visual—giving it a higher open-rate chance. Typically, your newsletter can be an "update" on what's gone on in the company for the past period of time. Some standard aspects a newsletter would touch on could be new hires; new partnerships; new customers/clients; an example of a huge success or "win"; any other exciting company news.

In terms of thought leadership, you could consider having a section entitled "A Note From Our [*insert your thought leader's title here*]." This would be an opportunity for your thought leader to write a personal, brief message, overviewing how the company's done for the last period of time. It's just another way to bring more visibility and awareness to your thought leader.

Earned Media

Now that you have the tools to effectively help your thought leaders position themselves correctly on owned media platforms, we can take it to the next level by pitching the media. When you pitch *earned media* you're connecting with real, legitimate journalists, who will only write about your client, or accept submissions, based on the merit of the pitch — not for any other reason.

Op-Eds

The most common form of thought leadership outreach in terms of thought leadership are op-eds. The term "op-ed" is one that dates back to the days of print newspapers. In the first section, the news section, towards the back there is typically an "Editorial" page—this houses the, you guessed it, editorials written by the staff. It's the one page on which the newspaper is allowed to share their opinion on a news story or pressing matter. Of course, that has changed drastically throughout the recent years, but historically speaking this is what the editorial page was designed to do.

The term "op-ed" stands for the *opposite* page from the editorial. This page houses submissions from non-newspaper staff to vocalize their opinions on a news story. This is the section to which you can frequently pitch your client, so long as they have a compelling and strong opinion on a news story. That's the most important thing to remember here—it's the *opinion* section, so make sure that your client is writing a piece that shares an actual opinion. Pro tip: the more provocative the opinion, or contrarian, the better—since it will increase the chances of getting the piece written.

As a first rule of thumb, determine the media outlet you are pitching your op-ed to. Is it a national newspaper or a local one? If it's local it's better have a local hook, e.g., "Local officials in New Orleans must do a better job when it comes to flooding". National op-eds can certainly have a local hook, but make it in the greater context of a national story, e.g., "The rampant flooding happening in New Orleans is a foreshadowing of climate change that will affect all of our American cities in the years to come."

Secondly, spend some time googling the "How to pitch the op-ed section" of the paper you're going after. They all have it and it's a great resource for you to review prior to discussing the process with your thought leader. This page typically will tell you how many words to make the op-ed, how to cite quotations, and other guidelines that the paper adheres to. It will also include the email address to send the op-ed to. What I like to do is to send it to the main email address (e.g., opinion@yournewspaper.com) but copy to the opinion editor (this can be found easily by googling the newspaper's name and "opinion editor").

Once the op-ed is submitted, give it at least 48 hours until you follow up. What's even better than a standard follow-up is if you're able to offer an even more timely news peg.

If you're lucky enough to have your client's op-ed published in a local or national newspaper, remember what we've discussed above and make sure to promote the piece on LinkedIn. In addition to this, ask your client to write a short post about the experience of writing the piece or why they chose to write it.

Letters to the Editor

Each newspaper also has a "Letters to the editor" section. In this section, readers email in their thoughts either on a news story or an editorial that the newspaper has previously published (likely from the day or two prior).

Sometimes, your client may not have enough to warrant a full op-ed (which typically start at 500 words). If this is the case, but they still make a point that's compelling, consider emailing in a letter to the editor. The same advice as the op-eds follows—research the section and what they look for. Each paper will have, again, its own slightly different requirements. When you research online, you'll also find the best email to send the letter in to.

Article Placements

Article placements, also known as contributed articles, are *not* opinion-based. This is when your client writes an actual news piece that goes in the newspaper, magazine, or website that you're reading. The only difference is that it's written by your client, who is not a reporter for that particular outlet.

Again, research the requirements for contributed articles, also sometimes called "guest submissions." Each outlet will have its own requirements, detailing what kinds of submissions they are looking for, and the length.

For this, and for all written materials, if your client isn't a natural writer you definitely will want to understand what resources you have available *before* you go down this road—especially if your client expects *you* to write these pieces!

An interchangeable term for article placements is "guest columns." Most editors will explain how you can pitch them effectively. You should read everything they've provided for those pitching them before sending anything to them. If you don't, you're jeopardizing your relationship with them before it's started. Most editors will have a very thorough overview of exactly what they look for and what they're interested in writing about at their publication.

Podcasting

A form of thought leadership that has really taken off in recent years is podcasting—both to pitch your C-suite as guests on various podcasts, and also to create your own. Creating your own podcast used to require an almost insurmountable amount of work and knowledge. Today, it is quite easy. You can find instructions for beginners online, and these are often tailored to your device: be that a smartphone, tablet, laptop, or personal computer.

Video

Video content is certainly the most technically challenging of all the thought leadership avenues to create and to create well. We all have iPhones and anyone can create a video—but that doesn't mean that you *should*. In particular, if you are creating a video of your founder or CEO it has to be of a professional-grade quality.

In today's fast-paced and competitive business landscape, establishing oneself as a thought leader has become more important than ever. Thought leadership promotes an individual's expertise and creates a distinct public profile for a company's leaders. It is a process that can help build a strong reputation and inspire innovation within an industry. Anyone can be a thought leader, but for the purpose of this chapter we need to focus on the C-suite executives of a company.

To be successful in the field of thought leadership, it is essential first to determine the industry and sub-industry in which that company operates. This requires a comprehensive understanding of the company's niche and a thorough analysis of the trends and insights in the industry. By doing this, PR professionals can help their clients present their thoughts on relevant news and trends within their respective fields.

While thought leadership is crucial for building a strong public profile, it also extends to a company's internal culture. A CEO's public profile can influence how employees view the company, how stakeholders perceive its performance, and how investors evaluate its potential. Therefore, aligning the company's internal culture with its public image is essential to establish a credible and authentic thought leadership position.

Summary

In conclusion, thought leadership is an integral part of modern business, and PR professionals must be skilled at refining and applying thought leadership tactics in their daily communications work. By understanding the industry and sub-industry, identifying key trends and insights, and aligning internal culture with external communication, PR professionals can help their clients establish themselves as thought leaders and stay ahead of the competition.

Pitching to Print Media

07

The first step in pitching the media is to figure out *what* you're actually going to pitch. Sounds simple, right? Actually, this can be a very challenging aspect, especially if your company doesn't have anything particularly newsworthy to report on at the moment. There are tricks of this trade, though, and this chapter should serve as a roadmap for getting your foot in the door with print reporters.

Let's take a step back. What exactly constitutes "print"? Back in the day, print *only* meant newspapers. Remember when newspapers had a morning and an evening edition? Yeah, me neither! But newspapers are what started the publicist-coined term "print."

The next iteration of print publications was the advent of magazines, both monthly and weekly. From women's outlets such as *Cosmopolitan*, to beauty magazines like *Allure*, to news periodicals like *Time* and *Newsweek*, there are hundreds of magazines published each month, with at least one in every topic area you could imagine (*Rider* magazine, anyone? A publication for you motorcycle enthusiasts).

The 1990s and early aughts were the heyday of print journalism. Why? There were many well-written print outlets in large circulation, making clients happy on two fronts if you were able to secure coverage. NYC publicists would rush to Hudson News to pick up a copy of the daily paper or the latest issue of a magazine, to marvel at their client's feature in print. Junior publicists around the country used to be tasked with bringing said print feature, and cover, to a framer to have the press placement memorialized in a beautiful frame to hang in the office.

Then, the internet was born. And, just like that, everything changed. With news available now at your fingertips, many didn't feel the need to buy a daily paper. Why spend the $5 on the new issue of *Vogue* when they could just read the news online?

All of us "old-school" publicists and journalists mourn the slow death of our beloved print outlets. Some of us remember the blood, sweat, and tears (and mostly late nights) that went into "putting a paper to bed" and being on deadline to "close an issue." Those were fun days, filled with hard work, looming deadlines, and teamwork.

The internet siloed reporters in an unexpected way. Prior to "digital," industry insiders only knew a handful of reporters by name, and only the really big ones—the ones who always had the scoop. Consider how much this has changed and evolved over the years. Presently, every single print journalist, at every single media outlet, has her or his own landing page, with a history of all their stories.

Going digital also sped up the *amount* of content being created. In the print era, a journalist might have filed one story a day, maybe no stories the next. Now, at some of the top digital news sites, reporters can file five or more stories *per day*. That's a ton of content, all with sharp deadlines. It has forced the reporters to work in their own world, without much collaboration with the rest of the staff.

But the digital era really helped us as publicists. Despite many newspapers and magazines folding, there are some that have survived. For even more, where the print version folded, the digital version not only survived, but also thrived. All in all, the creation of the internet engendered more opportunities, more outlets for publicists to get their clients press.

This is a good thing! More outlets mean more opportunities for clients and ultimately more press placements. However, it also creates more work. Which leads us to the first step in pitching print media.

Research the Print and Digital Outlets That Make Sense for You

The first step in pitching print and digital media (and really any media for that matter) is to identify which outlets are the most relevant to your industry. If you run comms at a manufacturing company, chances are slim that your business would make a good fit for

Men's Health. Similarly, if you work at a healthy food brand, you probably won't have much luck pitching *US News & World Report*. Hopefully you're picking up on a theme here.

"But, Annie, I have no idea which outlets are relevant for my industry. Help!"

I can help, and by using just one word: Google. Take to the internet and start researching. Do a simple search like this: [*industry*] + media outlets. For example: "beauty" media outlets or "tech" media outlets. This should start to give you a very broad scope of articles to read (a lot of "listicles" will appear) and some of the actual publications themselves will pop up (e.g., TechCrunch and Allure).

Spend time going through them. Read as many articles as you can. Then, start building a list. Most publicists utilize Excel spreadsheets, so that you can reference various tabs at the bottom. Start your first tab with the word "General." Populate it with as many of these mainstream outlets relevant to your industry as possible.

Next, do this Google search: [*industry*] + trade publications. For example: "public relations" trade publications. Or "legal" trade publications. This will pull up outlets like PR Week and Law360. Create a new tab at the bottom of your spreadsheet labeled "Trade," and start populating with these new outlets you've discovered.

Next, do a search on the local and regional media outlets in your area. What's your closest newspaper? How many newspapers are in your coverage area? What about magazines? A simple Google search of [*state name*] + magazines should give you what you're looking for. When I searched NJ magazines, a total of 28 popped up. Jackpot! Next... you guessed it. Add all of those contacts to a tab called "Local."

You have now created the beginning of your media list. Now, it's time to refine it.

Research Who You Are Pitching To

As basic as this sounds, it's a refrain I utter over and over again to my colleagues and when I'm teaching: "Research who you are pitching to." As previously mentioned, a simple Google search will pull up a plethora of information on the reporter you're trying to learn about. It's best to always start with a Google search, then read at least a few of her or his most recent articles. After that, spend a little time on their social media. Twitter is the platform most used by journalists, so start there. You'll be able to pick up on insights into the reporter by doing so, i.e., he may rant about something that's bothering him, he may have given a shout-out to his favorite sports team or he may be re-tweeting some of his favorite folks to follow.

All this does is provide you with clues about the person you're about to send a cold email to. This is going to give you a competitive edge if you construct your email in a way that lets the journalist know that you care and have spent some time sending a note that will actually be worth their time, as compared to the robotic pitches sent from Cision.

Remember: Print and digital journalists receive *hundreds* of pitch emails every single day. You need to make yours stand out! To that point, many journalists are now creating a unique link specifically for publicists, that aide in pitching efforts. My two favorites are from reporters who list extremely useful facts like contact information, what questions not to ask, what topics they find worth covering, and a response timeline.

Constructing the Pitch Email

First, always email. Let's face it, no one likes to receive a phone call out the blue, *especially* a reporter. The only time I ever call a journalist is if I know them well enough to pick up the phone and say hello or if there is a major story or scoop that's either sensitive in nature or that I am certain the reporter will be pleased to hear about. Otherwise, always email.

Second, remember that the person on the receiving end of this email is a person, too! This individual isn't going to want to read something that is too formal or that goes on and on, paragraph after paragraph. The reporter is probably quite busy doing their job, and even busier deleting irrelevant emails. Get to the point. Remember this adage as you write the pitch: What am I trying to sell and why should the journalist care? And it's not just the reporter you're hoping will care. You also want to highlight why the reader at home will care about this particular story. You just have to dedicate yourself to reading and reviewing the recent pieces by the journalist you're about to pitch, and potentially even reading some of the comments after each story. This will give you enormous insights into what the readers loved and hated.

Next, write the pitch. Now that you've done your research on the style and tone of the outlet and reporter; you've followed her or him on social media and gained some personal insights, you should be ready to write your own pitch. My advice on your first outreach is to keep it really short and simple. I like to start with a "Hi" before the first name as your greeting. Some prefer to just type the first name and put a dash or comma after it. Either way is fine—go with what is most natural to your own voice. Avoid saying "Dear" or "Greetings"— again, remember, this is a real person, just like me and you, on the receiving end!

You may want to continue with a brief introduction, something along the lines of:

> I wanted to introduce myself.
> I [insert very briefly what you do and why it's relevant to what he or she covers].

You could say:

> I run a local bakery and want to introduce myself since I know you cover local restaurants.

Or:

> You don't know me, but I'm a big fan of your work. And, since you routinely cover cars, I want to invite you to my antique car show next weekend.

If you really feel the need to go even more in-depth, you can always write the following:

> If you're interested, I've copied some more info on my organization below.

Do not put all the information you have into the actual email. Folks just do not have the attention span to read a long email, so if you have a full press release, or more detailed information to share, do so after your signature—so your email can be clear and concise at the top. Under no circumstances should you send something as an attachment. That's an automatic delete for most journalists.

You can end the email with a genuine attempt to try to keep the conversation going. Some examples:

I hope you'll consider me a resource in the future.

Anytime you want to visit my shop, I'd be thrilled to host you.

I'm often in your area. Would love to take you to lunch so you can meet my client sometime.

Then, finish up with some brief flattery. You may be scratching your head right now, thinking "I have to flatter this journalist now, too!?" The answer is "Yes." Remember, the relationship between publicists and the media is not 50/50. It's not even 75/25. You literally need to give 99 percent, and the 1 percent you get back is if and when a tremendous piece comes out about your client. Print journalists do not get paid a lot of money, and usually they have crummy hours and could, potentially, be poorly treated. The adage of the grumpy journalist isn't based on lies, it is, unfortunately, rooted in some truth. So, try to truly be that resource to them.

Personally, I think it works best if you can reference a story that he or she has written and pull out one specific aspect that really moved you, for example:

When you introduced Frank into the piece, it made me think about my own experience with my former boss, but in a way I had never realized before. Thank you so much!

The Follow-Up

You've written the perfect pitch. You press send. You wait. Now what?

I generally like to give at least a few days before I follow up. What I think works best is to reply-all to the original email, with a very quick follow-up note. It's best to reference that you're following up, but add in a bit of new information. For example:

> I wanted to check in on the below. Given your recent reporting on start-ups, I figured you could be really interested in the data I sent, which is all about the rate of success of start-ups.

Or:

> I read your recent piece on maritime fishing and I wanted to make sure you received my original email. We run a SaaS company dedicated to the industry and if I can ever be helpful with interviews or story ideas, I'd love to connect!

Don't just say "I'm just making sure you received my note" or "I wanted to check if you're interested in my pitch." The follow-up has to be more than *just* a follow-up. It has to be another way to keep the conversation going and hopefully getting the reporter interested.

Don't be surprised if you don't hear back. Unfortunately, the response rate is very low to cold emails. The most important to thing to remember about following up is to be genuine and authentic. Sometimes, I'll send a note to a reporter that *doesn't* include a pitch. It'll just say something to the effect of "I read your recent story and I really enjoyed it. Your stories are so insightful." You need to try to become a recognizable name to the reporter. This reason alone is a big deciding factor into why companies hire outside PR agencies— for their connections.

Once you get name recognition with the reporter, you will have a much better chance of breaking through the noise. When I was a producer, I would get hundreds of pitch emails every single day. I would delete 99 percent of them. The ones I kept were from folks I knew and names I recognized. Those, I always read and replied to.

So part of your follow-up needs to include trying to get to know the journalist. The first and easiest step here is to make sure you have and do read their recent work. This will give you clues into what types of experts they interview for their stories (i.e., he always wants to have a lawyer to substantiate an aspect of his story, or he likes to get "real people" to weigh in on the issues he covers). Once you start to recognize these patterns, you can more accurately pitch the reporter with the type of expert they will be interested in hearing from.

Next, you'll want to follow the journalist on social media. Yes, you've already glimpsed at her or his social pages to gain more insights prior to pitching. But now, you'll want to follow so you can routinely get updates on the reporter, but also to start commenting or re-sharing or re-tweeting. Every journalist is her or his own brand, and the more followers they have, or the more times a story gets re-shared or clicked through, the better the story performs, which means the more advertising dollars the outlet can pull in, which in turn makes the reporter more valuable to the corporation.

Journalism used to be less of a big business and more about, well, the journalism. It still is, but it's changed a lot. A reporter can write the best story ever, but if it doesn't get a ton of click-throughs or perform very well, editors and those in the C-suite will take notice.

When you comment on social media, people notice. And so will the journalist because... they're people, too! If you start commenting frequently, but with genuine, authentic, and insightful comments, the journalist may start to notice. Then, when you email them later on, the reporter may be more likely to remember your name, thus increasing the chances of him actually reading your pitch and reply-ing to you.

Try to figure out if there are any events coming up where you might be able to meet the reporter. Face-to-face interactions will always do wonders when you're trying to "get in" with the journalist. If your company is having a fancy party or hosting an event with an A-list speaker, use that as an opportunity to invite the journalist to attend. Remember, your interactions with the journalist don't have to be transactional... In fact, it's probably better that sometimes, they are absolutely *not* transactional. Building a relationship only works if it's done so in an authentic way. If you can develop a natural rap-port prior to you starting to pitch stories, even better.

Setting Up the Interview

The best thing ever has happened—the journalist got back to you and wants to set up an interview with your boss. *Yes!!* But... now what do you do?

First, do a little happy dance in your office to celebrate. Landing your first interview is a huge deal and you should feel proud. Next, make sure to get all the specifics from the reporter about how he or she wants to proceed. Do they want to do this in person? If so, where? Or do they prefer to conduct the interview over the phone or Zoom? Could it be an email interview instead?

You do have some leeway here, insofar as playing a part in the logistics of the interview. Personally, I think an in-person interview always works best. It allows the journalist and interviewee to talk in a more natural way, and if the interview is conducted on site at your company's business, your boss may feel more at home and at ease during the interview. Work with your boss, prior to responding to the journalist, to ascertain if he or she has any preference when it comes to these logistics.

If the interview is going to take place at your company's head-quarters, take some time to figure out which location is best. Do you want the interview to take place in a conference room, or is a more intimate setting, like your boss's office, more appropriate? Before the interview takes place, do you want to take the journalist on a tour of the space? You can always ask the journalist if he or she would like to speak with any other members of the company, or any of your customers/clients, if appropriate. This would give the journalist more color for the story and show them that you understand how putting a story together works.

As a publicist, you have a right to do this, and it wouldn't be weird at all for you to sit in on the interview. Most of the times, this is not necessary, especially if the subject of the interview isn't sensitive in nature. You may, however, want to consider recording the interview. I've had multiple times in my career where the journalist writes the story one way, and the client does not remember it in that exact manner. If you have a recording to play back, this alleviates any potential discrepancy that may occur.

Have some coffee or water available and offer it to the journalist. If there is an event coming up that you could extend an invitation to, now would be a good time. Make the journalist feel welcomed. Thank them for coming and ask if you can do anything to make their life easier.

After the journalist leaves, he or she should give you a sense of when the piece will be written. If the piece doesn't come out on the day they originally said it would, it's OK to send a quick note asking when the piece might be published. Once the piece does come out, make sure you read it first to check for any misspellings or factual errors. Double-check that the company name and your boss's name are spelled correctly. Then, give it to your boss to read. Make sure that he or she is happy. Ask some of your colleagues, friends, or family to read the piece to get their take on it. If everyone agrees it's a well-written piece, you should then make sure your directors or, if applicable, your investment company read the piece, too. Any key stakeholders who have a vested interest in the company will definitely want to receive and read the piece as soon as it's published, in case there are any errors that need changing.

After everyone is happy with the piece, be sure to liaise with your marketing, SEO and social media departments. Ideally, the news should be front and center on your company website's home page, for starters, with the logo tear-out at the top. Ask your marketing department what their plans are for promotion, i.e., will it be included in your quarterly newsletter? And make sure your social media team is well aware of the piece and is checking the outlet's handle and the reporter's handle to re-tweet and/or re-share. They will want to also make sure that several of their own posts/tweets/stories are going up as well.

Summary

The evolution of print media from newspapers to magazines and now to digital platforms has changed the landscape of public relations and journalism. The shift from print to digital media has brought about new challenges for publicists but has also created more opportunities to get their clients press. The abundance of online publications has made it easier for publicists to pitch their clients' stories and reach a broader audience.

However, pitching the media is still a challenging aspect of public relations, especially when a company does not have anything newsworthy to report on at the moment. In such cases, being creative and strategic in pitching the media is important. As the chapter highlights, knowing the publication and the journalists you pitch to is key to securing coverage.

The rise of digital media has also changed the way journalists work, with tighter deadlines and a need for more content. This has resulted in a siloed work environment, where reporters work independently and without much collaboration with the rest of the staff. Publicists need to understand these dynamics and adjust their pitching strategies accordingly.

Overall, the shift from print to digital media has brought about both challenges and opportunities for publicists. While the days of rushing to pick up a copy of a magazine or newspaper to marvel at a client's feature may be gone, the digital era has opened up new avenues for getting their clients press coverage. It is now up to publicists to adapt to this new reality and use it to their advantage.

Pitching to Broadcast Media

08

In my early years of agency experience, broadcast television appearances started as, continued, and to this day remain *the single-most sought-after media exposure* for nearly all of my clients. Even when we take on new clients who don't necessarily want to incorporate TV into their media strategy, nine times out of ten when presented with the opportunity to appear on a local, streaming, or certainly national network, they jump at the opportunity. Furthermore, and much more importantly, the outcome nearly always exceeds expectations.

Here's an example. We booked Paula Ratliff, the CEO of the organization Women Impact Tech, on a national business news network morning show not too long ago. Our pitching had been around Women Impact Tech's annual NYC event, in which young women in tech gathered to listen to inspiring and helpful leaders in the space speak, as well as to network with others in the field, all in the hopes of promoting job growth and opportunity for women in the technology field. We had done a ton of pitching on the event—mostly to digital tech reporters who might be interested in covering the event, but also to local NYC media, who often like to be informed of big events taking place in the city.

We were successful on both fronts, and secured local NYC coverage as well as tech reporters who attended, and then covered the event. However, that big national press placement still eluded us. So, we turned our pitching strategy to align Paula as a thought leader and subject matter expert on a story that, at the time, was getting a ton of traction in the media.

New York City passed a bill in recent years that requires companies within the city to include their salary ranges when posting for job openings. It was making a lot of news and was included as a top story of the week in most major media. Some experts were praising it—others were naysayers. Our client, Paula, thought it was a brilliant move, as for women in the technology field, who nearly all of the time earn less than their male counterparts, this new bill would allow them the chance to ensure they were interviewing for a position that was commensurate with their years of working experience. This was our chance to capitalize on getting Paula her first big national TV appearance.

I'll share with you here exactly how we got it done. First, I emailed the producer—who I knew slightly from having booked another one of my clients—about the event. Here's that pitch:

> NYC's salary transparency law takes effect this week, helping provide wage clarity to job seekers across the city. Wage transparency has been an ongoing issue in the United States—especially for women in tech, with female managers making as much as 10 percent less than their male counterparts.
>
> Paula Bratcher Ratliff, President of Women Impact Tech, can address NYC's newest legislation, which will help combat gender and pay inequity in the industry.
>
> Paula is in NYC this week for Women Impact Tech's Accelerate conference—convening hundreds of women, including female tech executives—from Peloton, Google, LinkedIn, Microsoft, Amazon Games, Tencent, Southwest Airlines, and more, and keynote speaker Reshma Saujani (CEO of Girls Who Code)—hosting sessions and panels discussing how they navigate their career in a male-dominated industry, overcoming Imposter Syndrome, equity in the future of work and more.
>
> I'd love to provide you with a press pass to the Accelerate and connect you with Paula directly. Please let me know if you're interested in attending!

As you can see, I started out with the big news of the day—the salary transparency law—and not the conference itself. You may be asking yourself: "But, wait. Isn't your job to promote the conference and help to draw awareness and attendees to the event itself? Isn't that the goal of your PR work with this client?"

The answer is *yes*. That's correct. And we had an entire team of colleagues working tirelessly to try to secure coverage that was singularly focused on the outcome of press placements *about this event*.

However, another objective of our media strategy for Women Impact Tech was to gain national exposure, positioning Paula as a thought leader and subject matter expert in the field. That's where this pitch and corresponding news peg comes in.

A couple other aspects to point out about this pitch. First, it's pretty short, right? For all pitching—but especially for TV pitching—you must keep your pitches short and to the point. Producers get not only hundreds of pitch emails to their inboxes daily, but also many emails from their internal team throughout the day. Their inboxes get clogged up! No one has time to read a really long email, and certainly no one has time to spend trying to figure out what, exactly, they are being pitched. Second, be clear about your ask. In the pitch above, I indicated that Paula was available to speak as a guest expert on the NYC salary transparency law, but also, I invited the producer (who I knew to be a young woman who often booked tech segments) to attend the conference. Either one would have been a "win"!

The producer responded a few hours later asking if the event was still going on tomorrow. *Yay!* A positive response! Only, wait… the event would be over by then. Now what should I do? I replied by saying that the conference ended today but offered the solution of having Paula available for an in-studio interview the next day.

This is what I like to call a catch-all response, meaning, I responded to her query about the conference and took it one step further by offering footage. I can't stress how important this is. I'm pitching TV, right? And TV is…. yup, you got it, a video-based platform! So, anytime you can include additional b-roll (video that is shown on screen while the anchor or reporter is talking over it), SOTs (sound on tape), where a roughly 30-second clip of your guest speaking is played), or footage, the better your chances are at securing a booking. Why is that? Because producers need visuals. For this example, it would be *highly unlikely* that a producer would book a segment about a conference without being able to show video from that con-ference. It wouldn't really be a segment at that point—it wouldn't even be a reader without video—because there would be literally nothing to show on camera without it.

A "reader" is when the anchor literally "reads" the teleprompter to deliver a bit of news, usually no more than 30 seconds. This read is almost always covered with b-roll footage of what the anchor is actually reading about. If you watch any of the major national morning shows, about 20 minutes into the show they almost always toss to the news desk, where that particular anchor reads the news. This news is, generally speaking, very important in the day's news cycle, but may not warrant a full segment—or perhaps they did not secure a guest on the topic, and therefore, moved the news into a "reader."

In my email response above, I reiterated that Paula would be available to speak on the pay salary transparency news story, and indicated that she could be in-studio, another way to sweeten the deal when trying to land a booking. Let me explain.

In the pre-Covid world, live TV interviews were done one of two ways: in a remote studio location or in-studio. It's important to note that most major TV media based in the United States feed from the hub that is New York, New York. A handful of shows are shot out of DC, but overwhelmingly they are in New York. So, what if you have a great client who just happens to live in Tulsa? Well, you would then have worked with the producer to book that guest out of a remote studio location in Tulsa. This used to happen all of time, and resulted in the "two boxes" you would see on the screen: the box on the left would be the face of the anchor, based in NYC; the box on the right would be your client, live from a studio in Tulsa.

As I mentioned, this used to happen all of the time pre-Covid, but it was starting to wane as standard protocol due to the expense. If your client was based in a top market, such as Chicago, Miami, LA, etc., the national network would certainly have a bureau in those cities.

A bureau is an official satellite office of a national TV news network that almost runs as its own business, led by a bureau chief, with an on-air correspondent, producers, and crews. The purpose of a bureau is to have resources in a location where there is often a need to cover the news out of that city.

Booking a remote studio for a guest in a bureau would essentially be free—or extremely low-cost—to the network. But when you have a client in a smaller city, like Tulsa, the network would then have to book either an often-expensive independent studio or their affiliate or owned and operated station, which can become pricey due to the cost of the uplink, and, oftentimes, hiring a crew at off-hours to staff and operation the station and interview.

Enter a post-Covid world and one amazing way that the pandemic has *helped* publicists in booking their clients on national TV networks is the proliferation of Zoom, Skype and other mechanisms by which guests appear on national TV from the comfort of their living rooms. The use of this technology really saved TV news in the first two years of the pandemic, allowing broadcasts to continue rather seamlessly, with the one difference of having virtually *all* of their guests remote, rather than in-studio. If you're pitching national TV currently, and your boss or client is *not* in NYC, then you need to use wording akin to this: "My client is available to join you via a remote studio in [*name of the city*] or via Zoom."

But, hands down, the absolute best interview in the eyes of the producer, anchor and your client, will be if it can be done "in studio," meaning just that—your client/boss is in the same studio as the anchor, sitting at the same desk. This allows for a much more conversational tone and banter between the two, which simply makes space for a more engaging, high-energy interview.

These days—and one of the main reasons why I indicated that Paula could be "in-studio"—the networks are moving away from Zoom whenever possible, but at the same time are still gun-shy about booking too many guests in remote studios. Why? The cost, of course. Just type into Google News "TV news layoffs" and you'll see a bleak recent history of national networks needing to cut costs, and, therefore, laying off staff.

Whereas I would classify print as a dying breed, I would position TV news as undergoing an evolution or a shift. There will always be TV news—but the vehicles by which we watch and obtain our TV news have already shifted so much in recent years, with certain shows being on demand or available on various streaming platforms. This makes the business of determining the network's profitability more challenging, as in a simpler world decades ago you only got, say, CNN on your big, bulky TV, courtesy of your local cable provider, and that network only made money based on the commercials—aka ad revenue—it would garner for each time slot. Today, there are myriad ways that TV networks can make money—but since it's still an evolution, none of them have figured it quite out, just yet.

Back to Paula—the producer replied saying that they were full for the next day's show, but could she join on Monday? I immediately replied (another important lesson—please reply to journalists, but *especially* to TV news producers—as soon as you possibly can. Don't leave them hanging! They may—and likely, will—book another guest while waiting for you to reply) and said she would be available, but would be back in Louisville, and asked if they would like to have her out of a remote studio or over Zoom. She replied that Zoom was fine, and on Monday morning Paula was live on a national business network.

The segment was focused entirely around the NYC salary transparency bill but Women Impact Tech got mentioned in Paula's intro, in her chyron (the text on-screen underneath a guest when talking; the chyron will state the guest's name and also their affiliation, i.e. which company they are representing) and, thanks to our coaching and media training, in one of her answers, when Paula very naturally weaved in the Women Impact Tech conference in NYC that had happened the week before, with some real anecdotes from attendees as to how they received the transparency bill news.

It was a fantastic segment, and after it was all said and done Paula told one of my colleagues that the interview and experience had been a "once-in-a-lifetime experience." It put a huge smile on our faces and also helped ensure that this client trusts us, recognizes the good work we do, but also saw the value in this national interview. As we'll get into in a later chapter, having the video clip of this national TV interview helped to boost their social networks and digital outreach as they approach and continue to engage with their various stakeholders.

This is just one example that clarifies a central thesis I have around TV news bookings, which I believe to be the most coveted of all media. There are *many* benefits, of course, to the other forms of traditional media (print, digital, radio, and podcast). For example, newspaper or magazine placements look fantastic framed and hung in your office. Digital articles can hyperlink back to your client's website, thus driving traffic. Drive time radio interviews have a very captive audience, with no distractions (unless you are someone who texts and drives—don't!). Podcast interviews tend to be much longer than radio interviews and allow the guest to really dive deep into her or his area of expertise.

But it's TV that I hear the most from our clients that they're looking for. TV has a certain cachet that just cannot be replicated in other forms of media. It can open doors in ways that your client may not have ever even thought of. It can lead to relationships, partnerships, and new career paths. But, most important, in the span of just three minutes you can reach millions, yes millions, of potential stakeholders… and limitless others with the coveted link of your client's appearance thereafter.

Before we dive further into the mechanics and tactics of pitching TV, I'd like to share a few additional stories that demonstrate the power of TV.

One of our legal clients, who shall remain unnamed, was seeking television placement at one point. Therefore, our sole charge for him was to book television appearances, wherein he could be positioned as a thought leader or a subject matter expert.

We were quite successful from the outset and continued to secure many national TV appearances each month. We targeted national cable networks primarily, such as CNN, Fox News, MSNBC, etc. On any given day, cable news shows tend to book on average one attorney per hour—meaning, there is a good amount of potential openings for booking your legal clients on TV.

A common practice implemented after each appearance was to work with this individual's web designer to take the link of each live appearance and populate it into the website's hopper (web speak for the center video portion on a home page). This person was and is very ritualistic about doing so, and always kept the home page totally up-to-date with his latest appearances.

This individual called me one day to thank me and credited our work in getting him a big new work opportunity. When I asked how, he told me that this external party watched the TV news appearances, liked and agreed with what this person had to say, and thus made the decision to reach out.

As my client said, "People see me on TV and think I'm a genius!" Guess what, folks? It's true. Not only is this individual the best of the best, but he also had a team who made him walk the walk.

People outside of a specific industry have no idea about everything that goes on behind the scenes to make TV magic happen. All they care about it is when they look up and see someone they know on TV, they are immediately impressed. They think: "Wow. This person must really be at the top of their field to get booked on CNN." And that may (or may not) be true. But one thing is almost universally true: without a great publicist in his corner, it is almost certain that he would not have gotten booked.

Another great real-life example to illustrate the power of TV is from a former client who is a medical doctor. She wanted to enrich her professional life and pursue TV as an option. We started working together and booking her on day-of medical news stories as they arose. She was a *natural* on camera, having undergone media training (more on this, later), and she immediately started getting re-booked quite frequently. After a shockingly short amount of time (less than one year), NBC News offered her the role of Medical Contributor. She holds this position to this day, years later. While a contributor title at a network does not mean you can quit your day job (the pay is great! But, for most, it's not enough to give up your full-time profession), it, once again, opens up many doors. This particular client has gone on to write books, enjoy paid speaking engagements, and secure lucrative deals with various brands looking for a prominent medical spokesperson. The power of TV is real!

But the most special example of the power of TV came from our work with a nonprofit organization. Thinking like a producer, we realized that the Thanksgiving holiday was just around the corner. We whipped up a pitch pegged to the day, with an intro along the lines of consumption surrounding the holiday.

That pitch (followed up with much more data), was enough to get a producer at a prominent network interested. The segment took place the day before Thanksgiving, with the anchor following a very similar intro to the pitch we had written. Our client was in the studio, sitting across from the anchor, and delivered passionate commentary about the struggles her organization faced in making sure no one went hungry again.

My client called me later that day to let me know that the office had received a call shortly after the segment had aired. The caller was so moved by the segment that, on the spot, they donated a large amount of money to the company.

So, booking TV segments sounds awesome, right? You are probably so psyched to start doing this for your company and you can almost hear the accolades and, hopefully, subsequent promotion for your good work. The flip side? Booking TV segments is extremely difficult to do. Out of all the forms of traditional media, it is, without a doubt, the most challenging to secure, for a variety of reasons. The first is that there is just not a ton of "real estate," so to speak. There are only so many channels, with so many relevant networks, with so many relevant shows, with so many guest openings. Second, *everyone* wants to get featured on TV. So, the competition is much fiercer.

When I was last a cable news producer, back in 2010, on average I would receive 200 pitches *per day*. That number has doubled, if not tripled, since. Imagine that—you're pitching your client to a producer who receives 500 pitch emails *per day*. Know what most of those producers do? Read each and every pitch and reply with a thoughtful message? Um, no. They hit "delete." You don't want to be deleted! So, let's get into it—how can you make your pitch stand out and secure that coveted TV spot?

Steps to Take Before Pitching

The first step before pitching TV, is to identify who from within your organization you want to put on TV. Is it your founder? Your CEO? Is it an employee who has a very compelling career journey? If it's for an event, who exactly do you want to give sound bites for the piece? When I say "identify," it's not just you in your head thinking, "Well, this person would be great on TV." You need to actually discuss it with said person. Make sure he or she understands what it involves. If you can, and if budget allows, strongly suggest media training.

The next step is to figure out what kind of broadcast is the most important to pitch and try to secure. Is local TV most important and aligned with your goals? Or is it national TV?

First, identify the types of broadcast that are important. Next, you need to conduct exhaustive research on those networks and drill down on the specific show(s) that are best aligned for pitching. This is done via watching as many clips or episodes of the shows as possible and getting a feel for the types of segments that are being done. Once you have this, you need to spend time thinking about the type of pitch you'll use when you conduct your outreach. Will it be a pitch about news within your client's organization? Or is it better to promote your CEO as a thought leader or subject matter expert in the space?

Once you figure that out, then you need to identify the appropriate producer to reach out to. This can be done by a simple LinkedIn or Twitter search. You want to find the "booker" or "editorial producer" on the show to email. Those are the producers who are responsible for finding and then booking guests. Most email addresses are easy to find as well. Once you find one person's email for a network, it's a safe bet that others will follow the same format. So, for example, if you see a jane.doe@network.com, it's a safe bet that her colleague's email is john.doe@network.com rather than jdoe@network.com or johndoe@network.com.

If you've never emailed a producer before, my suggestion is to keep your initial email very brief. First, you guessed it... research that producer! Nowadays, social media offers us a non-creepy glimpse into the person we are cold-emailing. Look them up, see what they're posting or tweeting about. Perhaps that will give you an idea for a more natural introduction. If nothing comes to mind, then reference an interview or segment you recently watched that you enjoyed—but be specific and say why you liked it (in one sentence).

Next, tell them who your client is and offer suggestions on how that client could become a resource for *them*. Booking TV news is difficult! It's a constant grind, with multiple hours to fill each week—

producers are always looking for "good talkers" that they can add to their rolodex. Mention your client and the various, relatable subjects that they can speak to. Offer up a news story but be sure to include your client's point of view on the subject. It's not enough to simply say "My client can speak to this news story." Tell the producer *what* your client would say on it, so that way they know what they're working with.

If you don't get a response, please don't send a follow-up note saying "Just making sure you got my email." Instead, wait for a time when you have a natural reason for following up... something that will pique their interest. Connect with and follow them on social media and try to start up a natural rapport. If you have a great event you can invite a producer to, try that! Remember, members of the media don't get into this industry for the pay. Most take their craft seriously, but at the same time they are humans who enjoy flattery and some of the perks of the industry—i.e. getting invited to cool events. Remember all of this when reaching out!

Media Training

Media training is just that—training and preparation for doing media, mostly TV interviews. Media training can and does take place for print interviews and it is often quite useful ahead of a speaking engagement or live remarks. But most of the time, when you hear the term media training, it's in reference to preparation for a TV interview, mostly for live interviews.

My biggest piece of advice, if budget allows, is to hire an outside media trainer, someone with real experience in this field. A simple Google search of the term will populate with multiple options. Despite your location, most, if not all media trainers, will conduct the training over Zoom. If asked, they may have consultants or freelancers they work with who live directly in your area. In-person is *always* best for media training. However, if it's just not possible, over Zoom or remotely will also work just fine.

If you just do not have any budget to hire an outside media trainer, then here are my tips for conducting a great training all on your own.

Understand the Type of Interview

First, be very clear on the *type of TV interview* your designated company spokesperson will be conducting. Is it live or taped? This is the biggest question to know the answer to.

A "live interview" means just that—it is live, and in real time. However, is it a live interview on-set, in-studio? Or is it a live interview at a remote location? Or will it be conducted over Zoom? If it's live, you need to understand that this comes with *much* more pressure to do well. There are no "do-overs" on live TV. Your spokesperson will either do a fine job or they won't. It's up to you to make sure that they are prepped and feeling good before the interview (more on this later).

If it's recorded, the pressure is off (a little bit). A recorded interview typically means that a reporter, or sometimes just a producer, will come to your client's location (office, home, etc.) and record sound bites that will later be turned into a taped package.

> A "taped package" is a taped piece that runs within a news program. Typically, a reporter sets it up and then "tosses" to the package. A taped piece can range in length but is composed entirely of b-roll footage, SOTs and standups from the anchor and tells the story of the news at hand.

Research the Outlet and Reporter Conducting the Interview

Your job is to prep your client/boss as much as possible so that he or she delivers a fantastic interview that gets the company's important talking points across, while also not feeling like an infomercial. A critical step in this process is to understand the network, show and reporter conducting the interview.

For example, if you book your client on CNBC and then the next week Fox Business wants to do an interview, there are going to be some pretty stark differences between the two, meaning, the ideology behind the network is vastly different. While *every* network claims to be unbiased, and we (hopefully) have reached the tipping point in terms of pandering to the left or the right, even with this course correction, there are still inherent differences amongst all the networks covering news. It's important that you know and understand these differences and can articulate them to your client.

Don't know where to start? Here's some tips:

- Watch the network your client will be appearing on. A novel concept, I know, but I can't stress how important this is. I'm not suggesting skipping work, staying home on your couch, and watching MSNBC all day. But, rather, log onto the network's home page, and start watching videos that they've posted throughout the day. You'll start to see patterns amongst the *types* of guests each network is booking, the *sentiment* from various guests and also the *conclusions* the anchors themselves are coming to after each interview. Simply watching several videos will tell you a lot.

- Read some articles. If you just type [*network name*] + audience into Google, countless articles will appear on their ratings, demographics, and highlights.

- If you can, if you know *anyone* who has previously appeared on these networks, call them up and ask them how their experience was. Nothing is better than real, first-hand experience to inform you of how, hopefully, your client's appearance will go. Don't know anyone? Feel free to shoot me an email and I will definitely give you my take on booking clients on these networks.

Now you need to understand the *show* your client is going on. Every network has a lineup with unique, live shows, sometimes starting as early as 4 am but certainly by 6 am, and they run sometimes until midnight. Usually in the wee hours of the night, re-runs are played (that sometimes draw a decent audience due to the West Coast feed). Again, let's pick some real differences here. If your client says a goal is to appear on a national morning show, and as a result of your pitching, both *Fox & Friends* and *Morning Joe* come to you and say they want to have your client on their program, you're going to have two *vastly* different interviews if your client were to appear on both.

My advice is pretty basic—watch the show. Review clips online. Read articles. Get as familiar as you can with the show.

Now that you know the network and the show that your client is on, be sure to ask the producer which anchor will be conducting the interview. I always ask this and frame it in a way such as "I'm just making sure that [*first name*] will be the one conducting the interview tomorrow." Anchors take vacations, so sometimes there will be a substitute. If your booking is on a morning show, typically there are several anchors who could, theoretically, be interviewing your client— be sure to know this information *before* you conduct your media training so you can ensure you'll be doing the best job possible.

Get as Much Info as Possible on the Topic

Here's something you need to wrap your head around: oftentimes, the segment you pitched and then booked is *not* the focus of the interview when the time actually comes. Why? Well, TV is a living organism and that organism changes with the news cycle. If a major story breaks an hour before your client's interview, number one, their interview may be canceled, or number two, you may receive an email from the producer asking if, in light of said breaking news, your client can speak to it as part of the segment.

While this is a very extreme example, it's important, nevertheless, to understand that, in all likelihood, the producer is going to care more about the actual *news* and less about what your client is there to *promote*. The producer may care about what your client is promoting *in relation to* the news at hand... but, ultimately, they care about making sure the viewer at home is getting "news they can use" and that is of the utmost relatability to them. Likely, this is not the small conference your client just put on, or news within your organization. This is where the media training really comes into play.

Ask the producer beforehand for as much information as possible about the segment. See if they will share some potential questions the anchor may ask, or if they have insights into the direction of the segment. Inquire if he or she will be conducting a pre-interview with your client. If the answer is "yes" listen in on that phone call so you, too, can be informed of the types of questions asked and answered.

My single most important piece of advice in media training is to make sure your client knows that, above all else, it's important to deliver an interview that the producer and anchor will be happy with. Why? Because then your chances of getting asked back are infinitely higher than if you bombed an interview—there's no coming back from that.

Taking it one step further, I want to clarify that it's more important to answer the questions asked and leave some of your talking points on the table. But, Annie, my client wants to be able to mention the big conference we just had or the news from within the organization. That's fine—but then you have to work really diligently in your media training to ensure that your client understands how to organically weave that information into one of their answers, and also understand that there's a good chance the anchor will not explicitly ask her or him about it.

You want to be able to forge a relationship with the producer. You want to be able to keep going back to her or him whenever there is a relevant news story to pitch. If your client gives an interview where all they're doing is talking about what's important to *them* and not staying focused or on track with the anchor, you will *not* be asked back and that relationship will not continue. Relay that to your client. What's most important is getting the video clip of the appearance afterwards, so that you can promote it properly.

Setting Up the Media Training

First, you need to figure out where you will conduct the training. In most instances, a conference room will work just fine—take your client out of her or his comfortable and familiar office setting, since they will not be afforded that comfort during the live interview. If you're able to hire an outside media trainer, chances are they may have their own studio in which they can simulate, very realistically, the interview process and feel. However, if you're doing this on your own, set up the conference room, table, and chairs as closely as you can to the way the set actually looks. You'll know this from watching many of the videos prior to the training!

Walk your client through the process from the beginning, and I mean the very beginning. Will they be getting to the studio on their own, or is the network sending a car service? If they are sending a car service, tell them to act as though they are on-air from the moment they open that car door. They must be polite and conduct themselves as though millions of people are watching—for soon they will be. Let them know they need to bring ID to be allowed into the building—after the sign-in at the front desk, either a guest greeter will bring them to the greenroom or reception will tell them exactly where to go.

The greenroom is one of my favorite parts of a TV interview, mostly because it's usually filled with so many interesting people: producers, hair and makeup artists, on-air talent, and other guests. I've had clients literally have partnerships formed down the road, based off of chance meetings in the greenroom. Get there early if you can and soak up the atmosphere! If the network will allow it, accompany your client—this is the place where you'll be able to meet other producers and the booker who booked this segment, in person. That in-person meeting is so important to solidify the relationship at hand.

Speaking of hair and makeup, make sure you understand completely if that will be offered to your client or if they need to come camera-ready. Camera-ready means that they have professional-grade hair and makeup when they arrive at the studio.

If your client is male, you have *far* less work to do here. Hair? They do that themselves. Makeup? They don't need any, maybe just some powder to reduce shine from all the bright studio lights. You can absolutely ask the producer if there is some powder available for your client to apply prior to the interview. Usually, the answer is yes. If the answer is no, consider investing in some. It will be worth it, in the end.

If your client is a female, you need to stress the importance of taking her appearance seriously. For first-time, on-camera guests, I strongly recommend having professional hair and makeup done. Through the proliferation of on-demand beauty apps, such as Priv, you likely can have someone come to you prior to the interview. However, make sure you're good on the timing—often, producers will want the guests to arrive at least 30 minutes before the live hit time. You also need to factor in the time it takes to travel to the studio location. Allow an hour for hair and makeup. So you may be looking at two to three hours prior to the live hit time for the makeup artist to arrive. You may get pushback from your client, who may not think she needs assistance, and that she can do it herself. That may be true! But there is actually nothing worse than having your client deliver a fantastic interview... only to have it be overshadowed when she watches the clip back and hates her appearance. Those studio lights *require* professional grade makeup. Trust me on this!

Next, walk your client through some of the basics of an interview. I love to start with good posture—no one likes seeing themselves slouching on national TV, though we all tend to slouch, don't we? One tip for ensuring you sit up straight is to put your butt all the way back in the chair. This will naturally force you to straighten your spine as you sit up nice and talk. Next, plant your feet firmly on the ground. For some unknown reason, many studios have swivel chairs for the guests! It looks terrible if you're swiveling back and forth. Planting your feet will ensure that you stay in the same position throughout the interview. Hand placement is a big one, too. I actually am in favor of *some* hand movement when talking—if that's something that comes naturally to you. It can't be too much, but I don't want a guest to be too stiff in stature, either. You want to conduct yourself as though you're having a professional business conversation or meeting.

Most importantly, train your client on *listening* to the questions asked. Inevitably, you're going to practice the talking points and messaging around what's most important to you and your client—but you need to have your client going into this interview *not* following a script. You need to throw questions at your client that are *not* related to their messaging points and see how they do. But, they can't just rely on your word for it—*record your practice sessions* and then watch them back with your client. Yes, this will be the cringiest thing you've done all year—but your client has to see, with her or his own eyes, how she does in a live interview setting—and the best way for that is to actually watch the tape back.

Remember, it is perfectly OK for your client to weave in their message points when asked a relevant question. But that needs to be done quickly and in the greater context of the subject at hand.

When you're watching the clips back, make sure to review your client's energy level. Normal energy does not work well for TV. A trick we like to do is to make your client talk like a game-show host (trust me, here) where they are ridiculously over the top in their answers. Then, have them scale that back 30 percent—that's probably the level of energy they need to have when doing live TV. Watch for filler works such as "ums" and "likes." Tell them it's better to take half a second to figure out what they're going to say, rather than stammering with filler words as they're working the answers out in their heads.

Prep them on what to do when the interview is over. Never just get up and leave after an interview. Tell your client to stay seated until someone on the set comes over to them to guide them off the studio floor. Make sure they thank the anchor. If the mood seems right, it is OK to ask for a photo—it's for promotional purposes, after all! It's a nice touch to send an email or hand-written note thanking the anchor and producer for a great interview, as well.

Remember, when it comes to media training and pitching broadcast media, to always revert back to this question: *What is your goal?* Is it overall brand awareness? Is it to promote a specific event? Is it to position your CEO as a thought leader or subject matter expert? By clearly understanding the answers to these questions, you will be able to pitch your client more effectively and to train them to the best of your ability.

Summary

As this chapter has shown, broadcast television appearances are highly valued by clients and their agencies. These opportunities often exceed expectations and significantly boost a brand's visibility. The success of Paula Ratliff's appearance on a national business news network morning show, discussed earlier, serves as a testament to this. The agency secured a coveted national press placement that had previously eluded them, through strategic pitching and leveraging Paula's expertise. My goal in writing about this was to highlight the importance of adaptability and creativity in media strategy. Although the agency had been pitching the Women Impact Tech event primarily to digital tech reporters and local media, they recognized the potential of leveraging the current news cycle to showcase Paula as a thought leader in the technology industry. By pivoting their pitching strategy and capitalizing on a top news story, they secured a valuable opportunity for their client. Furthermore, this illustrates the power of broadcast television in reaching a broad audience and establishing credibility for a brand or individual. Even clients who initially may not have been interested in incorporating TV into their media strategy often jump at the opportunity to appear on a local, streaming, or national network.

This should provide valuable insights into the importance of broadcast television appearances in media strategy, and the creativity and adaptability required to secure them. It underscores the significant impact a well-placed TV appearance can have on a brand's visibility and credibility, and the importance of remaining agile in adapting to the ever-changing news cycle to secure valuable media opportunities.

Securing Speaking Engagements

09

Now that you've successfully (hopefully) learned and mastered the earned media approach, your clients may start asking you about public speaking opportunities and if it's possible to turn great media placements into (paid) speaking engagements. It is possible, but the approach is slightly different than the tactics to take when pitching the media.

Speaking engagements allow the speaker to connect with their audience in a very different manner than being quoted in a digital article, or even giving a TV news interview. Live, in-person speaking events are typically done in front of an audience. In this post-pandemic world, the thought of live events and speaking in front of an audience may feel somewhat strange or even start to produce some anxiety. Feeling nervous is actually a good thing before you get ready to speak—it means you care, you're taking it seriously, and that you're feeling just nervous enough to want to do a great job and give a compelling talk to those who showed up.

A big difference between speaking in front of a live audience and doing a media interview is the length of time given. A TV news interview is typically between three and five minutes long, and a print or digital interview is mostly going to be whittled down into a handful of quotes. When you're asked to speak at an event, whether it's a large conference or to a private group, typically, the length is anywhere from 30–60 minutes. This is an incredible amount of time and provides an opportunity that is very different from earned media... but it can still *get* you earned media. Let me explain.

Many events will have reporters, producers, and various members of the media in attendance. One of the largest events in the United States is the Consumer Electronics Show (CES), which is held every January in Las Vegas. The number of attendees varies year to year, but it's always in the tens of thousands. The number of media attendees also varies, but is always in the thousands. Think about that! If you are lucky enough to get asked to speak at CES, you'll have the potential opportunity to connect with *thousands* of members of the media while you're there. And I don't mean just those who attend and listen to your talk—every event furnishes a "press list" and as a speaker, you would have access to this list (if you don't, just ask your point of contact who booked you as a speaker). The press list would include the reporter's name, the outlet they work for, and their email address. I always advise clients—and my staff when they're working with a client at an event—to obtain the media list ahead of time and spend as much time as needed going through it and figuring out the key media you'd like to get introduced to. It's a good idea to send an email to those key media members *before* the event, to start to develop a rapport with them. I'd recommend inviting them to your talk, but in the event they can't make it, ask them if they'd like to meet for a coffee or a drink while you're both in attendance. Being on the ground with a member of the media, meaning when you're in the same location, makes it much easier to actually get that face time… and for the journalist to agree to it!

Additionally, during and after most conferences, media articles and coverage come out about the event. If your client is a speaker at the conference, the likelihood of them getting mentioned in an article about the event is definitely increased.

Another huge difference between having your client speak during a TV or digital/print interview and speaking at an industry or related conference is the audience. During a media interview, the audience is the viewer or reader at home. The questions and focus of the interview will be tailored to that specific media outlet's audience. Your job as a publicist is to work closely with your client to ensure that they can easily strike a balance between getting their own messaging across, while remembering the audience (who are unlikely to be experts in your client's specific industry).

When your client speaks at a conference or private event, while of course you still need to be cognizant of the audience in attendance, there is a much bigger opportunity to connect directly with prospective clients and customers. At industry events and conferences, attendees *want* to geek out about news within the space. They are paying money to hear the speakers and many even bring notebooks or laptops to take notes, or to record the sessions. It's a learning experience for many, and for the speakers it's an opportunity to connect with the audience in a very special and meaningful way.

As with prepping clients for media interviews, you absolutely want and will need to prep your client for any live speaking engagement. Certainly, there will be parameters around the focus of the talk and, above all else, it's most important, in my opinion, that the event organizers walk away from your client's session feeling pleased with their decision to ask her or him to participate—this way, they can be asked back again in subsequent years. But there's another aspect to live speaking events that can be truly transformative for a CEO: building trust.

The audience at speaking events is going to be much more informed about the speakers and their areas of expertise than a cable news audience is about a guest in a live interview. A large portion of the audience at conferences work in that specific industry already. Chances are high that when your clients speaks at a conference, a large portion of the audience *already* knows who he or she is. And if they already know who your client is, there is also a chance that they have a preconceived notion, or opinion, of your client. Either way, a speaking gig offers a chance to connect with that audience in an authentic and genuine manner, with another huge sliver lining—it can lead to conversions or sales.

In PR, as we've already discussed, even the best of earned media coverage doesn't *necessarily* lead to an increase in sales. At conferences, and even more specifically at industry events, if your client has the opportunity to speak, there is a very strong possibility that he or she is going to receive one or more follow-up emails, looking to connect, or explore partnerships, or find a way to work together. So, by first delivering a fantastic talk, you will be ahead of the game in establishing that trust.

Booking Speaking Events and Conferences

Booking a speaking engagement isn't technically an earned media placement, but increasingly, more and more clients are wanting to round out their PR efforts with the opportunity to speak in front of desired audiences.

Going about booking a speaking gig (and hopefully a paid one at that... more on this later) can be an arduous process. Again, as goes most aspects of PR, there's no precise manual to follow for acing this process, but there are some tactics that should hopefully help to make this work a bit more streamlined.

1. Determine Which Type of Opportunity Your Client is Looking For

Since there are so many potential opportunities for speaking, it's a good idea to start off by being as specific as you can in determining which types of venues your client would prefer to speak at. As with earned media pitching, first revert back to the goals—what is the hopeful, intended outcome of this speaking engagement? This should be your driving force when determining which types of event are best suited to your client.

Then, go deeper. Is it better to target industry conferences, which may have a smaller but more relevant audience, or larger scale events, to get your client in front of as big of an audience as possible? Does it make sense to target various non-profit organizations, or perhaps colleges and universities? Are there specific businesses you'd like to tap into, or perhaps clubs? Does your client want to travel or stay local for these opportunities? All good questions when going through this process.

A NOTE ON TED

A popular route for speaking is to apply to give a TEDx talk. TEDx talks happen in cities all over the United States and are thematic. Being asked to give a TEDx talk increases one's credibility and legitimacy, as TED has made a name for itself as a trusted organization for putting out thought-provoking programming. If your client is interested in developing her or his own personal branding, this is a great place to start—although it can be quite challenging to secure a spot.

If securing a TEDx talk is a goal of yours, here are a few tips specific to the TED brand that are likely to help:

- You need a standout idea. This can be difficult to hear—or to relay to your client—but there's a good chance that your first idea is not original or compelling enough to attract the attention of event organizers. Do an exhaustive search on your topic on TED's YouTube page. You may be surprised to see that it's already been covered. If this is the case, you need to keep pushing the envelope. How can you progress the idea forward? What's a new spin you can take on it to show organizers that you're moving the needle on the conversation?

- Spend time mapping out an outline of your idea. Typically for TEDx, or many other types of speaking opportunities, you need to have a strong personal story to lay out the basis for your talk. You want to also make sure you have takeaways for the audience, but with absolutely zero salesy element to it. TEDx talks are not meant to "sell" a product or a service—the brand recognition your client will undoubtedly receive from speaking at an event will be all you need. When you have your big idea, record it. Some event organizers will require a video of speakers, to check to see how well they can deliver in front of a live audience—but it's also a great exercise to ensure there is enough meat for a five-minute presentation.

- Apply six to eight months *before the event*. Each conference has its own deadline entry and process, and TEDx is no different. If you don't apply within the timeframe given, which is usually around six months, you won't be given a chance to be considered by the judges.

- Apply locally. This means—apply to any local TEDx conference where you have a connection. Think about where you grew up, where you went to college, places you've lived and anywhere within a reasonable distance from where you are currently located.

- Memorize, memorize, memorize. All TEDx talks are given from memory—whereas at other speaking engagements you may be able to have notecards or a teleprompter. And since each talk is roughly fifteen minutes long, that's a lot to memorize!

- If at first you don't succeed, try, try again. TEDx talks are amongst *the most* competitive to be accepted into. You probably will not get accepted on your very first try. That's OK. Keep at it and keep refining your ideas and keep applying.

2. Build Out a Calendar of Events

This is probably going to be the most time-intensive aspect of any speaking project. First, start with the locations. Take your city, your state, and then a broader region to start. We all use Google on a daily basis—this is no different.

Doing simple Google searches should help you to populate a calendar or a spreadsheet—whatever is easiest for you to keep track of all of the events. Start by going broad with a search such as: "Top speaking events in [*insert your city, state, region*]". If you are a fitness instructor, then Google "[*city name*] fitness conference." Start trying different variations of this and you will begin to have a fairly robust media list.

You can also check out industry trade publications to see what events they are promoting within the magazine. It might be a good idea to also look into local colleges or universities so you can get a sense of all-college events, but also various department events that you could be a good fit for.

Another easy way to find more conferences is to use various hashtags on social media. Some examples can include: #conferences, #speakingengagements, #liveevents. But then you can get more specific with something like #[*city name*] events or #[*industry*] conferences.

Likely, there are other industry experts or speakers in the space—you should start following them on social media. See what they are promoting on their LinkedIn and this may give you some good ideas. It's fairly easy to find the bigger conferences—the ones that have name recognition. But there are myriad private companies that will—either from time to time, or quite regularly—bring in speakers as a form of teambuilding or to offer advice to the staff. Following your favorite speakers online may give you some of those ideas.

If there are some that you feel comfortable approaching, think about sending them a direct message to ask them about their experience speaking at the conference. Networking is a big part of how you'll find future speaking opportunities—so try to put yourself out there as much as possible when it comes to speaking events.

Of course, you'll want to focus on the events that are coming up within six months so you have a shot at being accepted as a speaker. But this will be an ongoing process, so eventually you'll want to develop a yearly calendar, along with submission deadline dates, so you can have an ongoing process of submissions.

Now that you have a fairly robust list of conferences, start delineating them into which ones you most want to speak at. Then, pick a few that are "reaches" and a few that are more likely, to start applying to. Go one at a time—but it will become an equation of how much time and how intensive the application process is versus the likelihood that you will be selected versus how much speaking at that particular conference will be helpful to your overall goals.

You should allocate time each and every week to searching for new conferences and speaking events and also for the application process. New events pop up all the time, and submissions will become available on an ongoing basis. You must dedicate time to this process if you want to be successful.

As with most things, you can put money into sourcing the most appropriate speaking events for you. If there is a budget within your company, this could be a good use of time, as finding and applying for speaking engagements can be *very* time consuming. The company IntelNgin has a speakers section that will automate this process for you in likely a fraction of the time it would take you to build it out on your own. But, of course, it costs money—so, again, it comes down to weighing the pros and cons of outsourcing this project versus doing it yourself.

I will say that when you are at a stage to outsource various aspects of PR work—but in particular speaking engagements—it can really be helpful because it will free you up to work on aspects of your job that perhaps you enjoy more or that bring more value to the business. People are sometimes shocked when I share that I retain an outside speakers agency to help book my own speaking gigs—but it's helped me tremendously both because they have secured me incredible gigs but also because I simply didn't have time to do it myself.

The agency I work with is called cred and they are so good at what they do. Based in San Francisco, they have clients globally. Here is a blurb on their site about how they work with me and Pace Public Relations:

> Pace PR utilizes speaking opportunities to position themselves as leaders in the PR and the communications industry. Working directly with Pace PR's President and Founder Annie Scranton, cred collaborated with her to develop her speaking goals, create a speaking platform, define her target industries, and generate unique topics that highlight her experience and expertise. Focusing on events in the PR/communications, women in leadership, and entrepreneurship sectors, cred has helped grow Annie's thought leadership presence and Pace PR's brand awareness in these spaces.

Next, they outline my goals:

> Raise Pace PR's profile as a leader in the communications/PR and entrepreneurship space.
>
> Build Annie's personal brand as a leader in women's leadership, PR, and entrepreneurship.
>
> Show Annie as a thought leader and create lead generation for Pace PR.

Then, they go into my speaking platform and they share the various talks that together we've ideated and then formed:

> Avoiding the 5 common PR pitfalls all entrepreneurs make
>
> The golden rule of building a relationship with media
>
> What's BYOP? 7 steps to being your own publicist
>
> Making the news: 5 steps to getting media coverage for your start-up
>
> Perfecting your pitch

Breaking the Glass ceiling: Why female executives need personal branding

From trials to triumph: How to rebuild after a setback
cred has done an incredible job for me, and has booked me, at this point, dozens of fantastic speaking opportunities such as INBOUND, PRSA Icon, Startup Grind Global, Ascent, Dig South, and many others. They don't work for free—but they are worth every penny.

There are also speakers associations you can consider joining. Speakers associations are large groups made of up individual speakers. The association then helps to find and secure paid speaking opportunities for you. One of the most popular in the United States is the National Speakers Association (NSA). But there are many, many for you to research and choose from.

The benefit of joining is pretty clear—you're going to have the manpower of an established group that will help you to find relevant and hopefully impressive gigs for you to speak at. But this also doesn't come free, so I'm going to provide you with some key aspects to consider if you're thinking about joining a speakers association.

First up—*the money*. To join a speakers association usually comes with membership fees and dues. Many times it's an initiation fee and then an annual renewal fee that can be in the hundreds of dollars. Make sure that you aren't wasting your time and are pursuing the speakers associations that work within your budget. These membership dues and fees are easily found if you spend enough time on Google.

Next, make sure you're selecting an association that is within the *appropriate geographic region*. There are many national associations in the United States but Canada has some as well, including the Canadian Association of Professional Speakers. National groups have their obvious advantages—more name recognition and thus more opportunities. But if you're a newer speaker, there is a chance you could get lost in the mix of speakers who have more name recognition. In that case, it may be more beneficial for you to select a local or regional association. Again, this all comes down to research, but one tip is that there are many chapters of NSA, focusing on states or regions, so this could be a great place to start.

On the other end of the spectrum, there are international associations to think about as well. If you are someone who travels internationally fairly often and like the idea of potentially presenting in an exotic location somewhere around the world then this could be a great avenue to explore—if, of course, your industry expertise translates on an international scale.

Once you've narrowed down your search to a handful of viable options, try to connect with speakers who are a part of that organization. Here is where you will get unfiltered truth about her or his experience with this particular speakers association. Ask questions you want the answers to. How often did they secure you a speaking gig? Did you get paid, and, if so, what was the range? Are they responsive to your inquiries? Are they proactive in sourcing new events and conferences?

Along these lines, spend as much time as you can on the association's website, to try to get a sense of the values they purport to have. Read testimonials. Try to find social media posts from past speakers. You want to make sure you're entering into a partnership with a group you are proud to be a part of.

3. Begin the Application Process by Researching

As you've probably picked up on by reading the previous chapters in this book, research is really the cornerstone of almost all good public relations practices, from earned media to securing speaking engagements.

Select the top five conferences you want to try to apply for, and start researching those conferences. Start by scouring their event website. Look at past video clips from speakers from previous years. Research what kind of audience attends. This will ensure that you put together a proposal that will resonate with the event organizers but also that it's the right audience for *you*. Ask yourself the following questions:

- Will the audience likely be filled with prospective clients and customers that you want to reach? Is the conference geared towards junior or mid-level professionals, or is it more of an executive track?

- Is this speaking opportunity earned or paid? Paid can be interpreted two different ways—some events will happily have you speak at their conference if you pay a sponsorship fee. If that's the case, you'll want to be crystal clear on the amount before you spend any other time on it. When you are just starting out, it will be unlikely that you'll actually get *paid* money to speak—but if turns out to be the case, that's wonderful!

- Are there any specific requirements the conference needs from its speakers? Meaning—do they ask for credentials or a video reel or past speaking experiences?

- Lastly, make sure you are clear about the application process and the dates for submission.

You may want to consider looking into which speaking events your competitors have spoken at recently. Some may think this is copying or cheating—but I say it's just a smart tool to add into your research process. Once you've identified conferences that your competitors have spoken at, you could even reach out to the event organizer by saying something along the lines of: "I saw that last year you invited [*speaker name*] to speak at your event. I have a presentation that really builds off of that topic and moves the conversation forward. I'd love the opportunity to share it with you." Sending a professional and polite email like this may not result in a confirmed new speaking engagement—but it certainly can't hurt.

One important piece of advice—don't copy your competitors. It's one thing to build upon their previous ideas and move the topic forward, but don't make your presentation a carbon copy. Remember— your reputation is everything and you don't want to be seen as an inauthentic person.

4. Contact the Event Coordinators

Now comes the application process. Certainly, follow the directions that are provided to you on the event's website. Complete that process and see if you can take it one step further. If a video submission is not required, think about providing one. Think of ways to make yourself stand out. There will likely be hundreds of other potential speakers who are looking to get the same spot you did—remember that and try to make your application stand out.

Once you've actually completed the speaking process, it's easy enough to find out the names of the individuals who are actually the decision makers along the way. If you're able to find their email address, send them a note. A message on LinkedIn would work as well.

I encourage this additional form of outreach because it shows that you care and are invested in the process. It's perfectly fine to say that you understand that the final decision will be made via the completed application process indicated on their website—but here is your chance to send a personal message, something to further let them see the human side of you.

Some ideas of what to say include: Have you attended their conference in the past? If not, do you know someone else who has? Definitely mention that and let them know the impact it made on you, or your friend. Pull out very specific moments to share. You don't want to only say something very generic like "Your conference was so inspiring." You want to maybe call out a specific speaker and a specific sentiment that resonated with you during the conference and that has stuck with you until today.

You need to make these as personalized as possible—and even for your full application process. It may feel really easy to copy and paste the same deck over and over again. But the more time you can spend up front making each submission as individualized as possible, the better your chances will be of being selected.

Also, keep this outreach brief. As we've mentioned in previous chapters, no one has time these days to read lengthy emails. Three to four sentences should suffice. Tell them who you are, why you enjoy their conference and what unique value you could add as a speaker. Extra points if you're able to look into the conference head's background and call out, in a germane and authentic way, something about their own background and experience.

It doesn't hurt to follow up, either, but do keep in mind that most submissions will be considered several months before the actual conference dates.

5. Attend as Many Conferences as You Can

While you're waiting to hear back to see if you were selected as a speaker, it's a good idea to try to check out as many conferences and speaking events as you possibly can. This should be done so you can get a taste of what a good speaker looks and sounds like on stage. Take notes—see what worked really well and start thinking about your own delivery and if there are elements from others' presentations that you can adapt into your own.

But attending conferences can also be a fantastic opportunity to mix and mingle with event organizers. When you get to the registration desk, take note of what color lanyard the event staff is wearing. When you then see a staff member, try to engage in conversation. Tell them how much you're enjoying the event and why. Tell them about your favorite speaker. Then ask if they have a card and tell them you were so happy to connect and you'd like to stay in touch.

When you do stay in touch, by sending a follow-up email, again… all roads lead to research! Find out where the organizer is based and look them up online so you're familiar with their background. Ask them if they'd like to meet for a coffee or if they'd be up for a visitor at their offices. Remember to keep it short and sweet—but you may want to offer up being available to provide a testimonial on how much you enjoyed attending the conference. They'll love that. It's all about providing value to the person you are reaching out to.

One other tip—when you're at these conferences, take a ton of photos and make sure you post them on social media with the appropriate hashtag. The more that they see you as involved in the community, the more likely they will be to respond to your emails, meet you in person, and entertain the idea of having you present as a speaker.

6. Make Sure Your Website and Decks Look as Good as Possible

After reading your submission, the first thing any event organizer will do is Google you. Inevitably, this will take her or him to your website.

Make sure it looks good and is presented in a way that will scream "Look at me! I'm the speaker you want!" Similarly, make sure your LinkedIn is up to date and has appropriate titles of where you've spoken recently in your bio. If you don't yet have a YouTube page, get one. This is where you can store any and all videos of yourself talking. Haven't been invited to give a speech yet? No problem— invest in yourself, a modest amount, and find a local studio and videographer for an hour and record a couple of your talks. Good editing will yield you a professional video that is meant to show just how invested you are in this process of becoming a serious and polished speaker.

7. Referrals, Referrals, Referrals

Good business yields more business and a *great* job at speaking will absolutely yield more customers for you—and more paid speaking gigs. This should be how you think about the ROI of putting yourself out there as a speaker.

Starting with getting more paid speaking opportunities, this will inevitably happen if and when you deliver a great presentation. Either there will be someone in the audience who will see you and reach out, or will tell someone about you and then they'll reach out. Additionally, most events put the video of their speakers online after the conference—those videos live forever on the web, and can and should serve as your future calling card as a speaker.

Taking it one step further, make sure you have access to that video *before* you deliver your speech—ask if you can get the original file so that you can upload it to your own YouTube page. It's important to get clarity on that prior to delivering your speech and not after. If for some reason the event organizers aren't planning to record your talk, ask if you can bring in your own videographer. Capturing the video of you talking will be so important as future event organizers who are considering booking you will undoubtedly watch those videos and have their decision swayed, hopefully in the right direction, once they see what a fantastic job you did.

But these speaking opportunities will also yield new business opportunities and new professional relationships that are very important to consider. Most people don't pursue speaking solely to get asked to speak again and again. For most it's an exercise in overall personal branding. Adding "speaker" to your résumé and actually speaking in front of a room filled with hundreds, maybe thousands, of people will absolutely lead to new and strategic relationships.

Which is why it's so important to remember the human element of all of this. People who will be in attendance when you're speaking are genuinely interested in what you're saying. So remember to be as genuinely interested in them right back. Folks will want to come find you after your presentation and thank you or ask follow-up questions. Be as gracious as you can be—first, because it's just the right thing to do, but second, because you *never know who you're talking to*. Some of these conversations can lead to opening doors you never even dreamed of.

I'll give you an example. I've spoken at dozens of conferences and events throughout the years and most of them have found their way onto YouTube. I did a video one year ago for my client, the Association of National Advertisers Growth Council. They do an annual Global Day of Learning and the video I recorded for them was entitled: "PR power: The importance of earned media for your brand." The video is about 22 minutes long and I talk about all of the ways in which I've seen earned media help a brand and some of the tactics I, and the others at Pace PR, implement to secure these earned media spots. Well, it was to my great shock and surprise when, more than a year after that video had been published, I received an email from a book publisher who said he had watched that very video and thought I could be a good candidate for writing a book. That would be this book that you're reading right now! Writing a book has always been a bucket list item for me, but I truly didn't think that speaking engagements would be the way in which I would go about securing a book deal. But it was! And this is just one case in point of how speaking can lead to all sorts of wonderful opportunities.

Remember, now that you're a speaker, to start telling people! Don't be bashful about promoting yourself. I am a firm believer that when you put the intention out into the world, there's a good chance it will come back to you and deliver. Start weaving the fact that you're a guest speaker into professional conversations. When you're about to make a point in a conversation, maybe mention that it was this very point that was the cornerstone of the most recent speech you gave. The others may then say "Wait, we didn't know you were a speaker!" Which is exactly what you want.

You can also start by sharing videos of yourself talking on social media and make a call to action, i.e., "If you're looking for a speaker at your next event, please feel free to reach out." Doing so will help you gain more exposure as a speaker and attract potential clients looking for someone with your expertise beyond in-person conversations. Most people have hundreds, if not thousands, of social media contacts that they don't connect with regularly. Posting a video provides the opportunity for people from your network who might not have previously known that speaking is another facet of your expertise.

Building relationships and maintaining a strong network can lead to more opportunities in the future. So go ahead and put yourself out there as a speaker—the more you promote yourself, the more likely it is that you'll get noticed and booked for your next speaking engagement.

Ultimately, public speaking engagements offer a unique opportunity for individuals to connect with their audience in a way that differs greatly from earned media. While media placements can help build credibility and increase visibility, speaking at conferences and events can provide a deeper level of engagement with potential clients and customers. With the potential for thousands of media attendees at conferences like the Consumer Electronics Show, speaking engagements also offer a valuable opportunity to connect with members of the media and build relationships that can lead to future coverage.

However, speaking engagements also require a different approach than earned media. Speakers must be able to engage their audience for a much longer period of time, typically 30–60 minutes, and should be mindful of the specific audience they are speaking to. Publicists should work closely with their clients to ensure they strike a balance between delivering their own messaging and catering to the interests and needs of the audience.

Despite the potential benefits of public speaking engagements, it is normal for speakers to feel nervous before taking the stage.

However, this nervous energy can be channeled into a positive force to help speakers deliver a compelling talk that resonates with their audience. By taking advantage of the opportunities that come with public speaking engagements, speakers and their publicists can build stronger connections with audiences and media contacts, ultimately leading to increased visibility and success in their respective industries.

Conclusion

As we come to the close of this book, we reflect on the crucial role of public relations in building successful brands. Defined as a strategic communication process that builds mutually beneficial relationships between organizations and the public, PR is what makes a company or brand visible and memorable amidst a sea of competitors. Its impact, however, is qualitative rather than quantitative, and it takes a skilled practitioner to execute it effectively.

Navigating the labyrinth of PR can be daunting, but this book serves as a beacon of light, offering a roadmap to success. As we delve deeper into the nuances of PR, we discover that there are many misconceptions about what it is and what it isn't. PR is not marketing, advertising, social media, or content creation, although it may be a component of these broader marketing strategies. Rather, PR is the art of maintaining a favorable public image through earned media, telling your company's story in a way that captures the hearts and minds of your target audience.

It's also clear that the public relations industry has undergone a seismic shift in recent years. Each of the preceding chapters has deftly illuminated the evolving landscape of public relations, underlining the pressing need for professionals in the field to be nimble and adaptable in their approach to new media formats and opportunities.

The transformation from traditional print media to the brave new world of digital media has thrown up both challenges and opportunities for publicists. To succeed in this fast-paced and ever-changing environment, they must summon all their creativity and strategic nous to pitch their clients effectively.

Moreover, it is not just the digital realm that publicists must navigate with deftness and agility. They must also be able to leverage the power of broadcast television appearances and public speaking engagements to enhance their clients' credibility, connect with audiences, and secure valuable media coverage.

The paramount lesson to be drawn from these observations is the importance of remaining adaptable and flexible in media strategy. The public relations industry is constantly in flux, with new opportunities emerging at every turn. To succeed, professionals must be attuned to these shifts, staying ahead of the curve and taking full advantage of every opportunity. By doing so, they can ensure their clients remain visible and relevant in a world where the media landscape is constantly in flux.

There is no one-size-fits-all strategy when it comes to public relations. If you ask ten different communications professionals to define PR, you're likely to get ten different responses. But when it comes to media relations, and more specifically earned media, there are various tactics that will likely increase your chances of success, which I've outlined in this book.

Ultimately, the success of any PR campaign hinges on the ability to secure earned media. This is the holy grail of PR, the ultimate prize that can elevate a brand from obscurity to stardom. While there's no silver bullet to achieving this coveted goal, proven tactics and strategies can make all the difference. This book explored crafting a compelling story, building relationships with key stakeholders, and securing high-profile media placements.

If you want to be successful at earned media placements, you need to find your own way of working, your own way of getting to know reporters, and your own way to let the creative juices flow as a means to the important end goal of secured coverage.

Of course, it's also crucial to understand the evolving media landscape and three spheres of influence in media—print, broadcast, and digital—that shape and inform public opinion. While digital media has transformed the communication paradigm, broadcast media, especially television, remains the king of media platforms. A well-executed TV segment can move the needle of public opinion in ways that digital or print media may find hard to replicate.

To navigate these mediums, PR professionals must remain flexible, adaptable, and imaginative in their approach to effective communication. The ever-changing media landscape requires an unrelenting commitment to staying informed, creative, and innovative to ensure a brand's message resonates with its intended audience.

An authentic and well-crafted origin story is more than a marketing gimmick; it is a masterpiece that tells the story of a business, its triumphs and failures, and its hopes and fears. It is a testament to the human spirit and a call to action that inspires and motivates. A powerful origin story transcends mere marketing jargon, connecting businesses with their customers on a visceral level, engendering trust, and fostering loyalty.

Before pursuing earned media opportunities, a well-crafted elevator pitch must be crucial to effectively communicate a brand's unique selling proposition. Creating an elevator pitch requires thoughtful consideration of a company's purpose, its differentiating factors, and the value it brings to its clients. In essence, a well-crafted elevator pitch can be the difference between successfully communicating a brand's value and failing to capture the attention of potential clients, investors, or the media. It is not a one-time exercise but rather a foundation for building a brand's messaging. Therefore, it should be reviewed and revised regularly to reflect company goals, services, or target audience changes. While this exercise can be done individually, collaboration with others in the organization, including managers, bosses, and colleagues, can lead to a well-rounded and compelling pitch that captures the brand's essence.

And we can't forget about how establishing oneself as a thought leader has become essential in today's fast-paced and competitive business landscape. Thought leadership promotes an individual's expertise and creates a distinct public profile for a company's leaders. It is a process that can help build a strong reputation and inspire innovation within an industry. To be successful in the field of thought leadership, it is essential first to determine the industry and sub-industry in which that company operates. This requires a comprehensive understanding of the company's niche and a thorough analysis of the trends and insights in the industry. By doing this, PR professionals can help their clients present their thoughts on relevant news and trends within their respective fields. Plus, while thought leadership is crucial for building a strong public profile, it also extends to a company's internal culture. A CEO's public profile can influence how employees view the company, how stakeholders perceive its performance, and how investors evaluate its potential. Therefore, aligning the company's internal culture with its public image is essential to establish a credible and authentic thought leadership position.

At the time of writing this book, the team at Pace PR is comprised of approximately 20 people. Just like many companies, we finish up each fiscal year with annual reviews for both the company and individual performance. These meetings are always an incredibly eye-opening experience. I sat in on every review and heard about my staff's own, unique ways for securing earned media coverage for our clients. Account Manager and Head of Broadcast, Natalie Medved, has a uniquely challenging role within the company, as she is managing several accounts while *also* running our TV department and lending her expertise, pitching, and hits for clients, company-wide. Her day starts around 7 am, by turning on the major national morning shows (*Today*, *GMA*, *CBS Mornings*) to see what the lead stories of the day will be. Those morning shows typically dictate the news cycle for the day, and the stories in the first hour will often be the ones that are told on the cable networks.

PR isn't an exact science—there is not a perfect manual that I, nor anyone, could give to you to ensure success. For you and for many PR professionals, it may be a series of trials and errors until you unlock the secret to your own success. Part of what is difficult to teach—and certainly to capture in words in this book—is how to read between the lines of a news story, meaning, what they *haven't* covered, what angle was *not* discussed. It's often this aspect of critical thinking and having industry expertise that can lead to a booking or an interview on the same story. To this same point, a publicist must always be asking themselves "What's next?" Meaning: what will be the next aspect of this story that will be told in the media? It's this forward-thinking approach that will get you your next earned media placement—not regurgitating the same story, with the same talking points that you've seen on TV that morning.

After Natalie and our other colleagues have watched the biggest stories on TV that morning, they immediately dive into reading the major newspapers and news sites of the day to get those perspectives. Think: *New York Times*, *Wall Street Journal*, Insider, CNBC, etc. A really great way to get all your news condensed into very easy-to-read formats is to subscribe to those outlets' various newsletters.

Every single media outlet has at least one—most have more than one, with specific focuses—and it's a real life-saver when you have a busy morning but need to make sure you're up on the news.

At Pace PR, we've created a "morning note," which we send out to various producers and reporters via Mailchimp. It's formatted to have the top five news stories of the day, along with a client who is equipped to speak on that topic. We include a link to the client's biography, along with a link to their most recent TV appearance (producers will rarely or never put someone on TV without seeing how they performed on TV previously). We have many producers who subscribe to the morning note and use it as a means to finding great guests to put on the air. But it does something else that's really important for our process. It sets us up for the day. At Pace, we have at least a dozen clients at any given time who can, and would like to, comment on day-of-news topics. Clearly, we can't pitch every single client, on every single news story, on every single day. Part of being a great publicist is knowing how not to annoy producers. It's a fine line of communication—being a resource to the media with great experts for them to interview—but if you over-pitch, or are perceived as pushy, you risk damaging the relationship. By creating our morning note and going through this process early each morning, we are able to identify the top stories of the day, while keeping us on track of what truly is best to send to the media.

That's a snapshot of what works for those in our TV department. It's wildly different from those on our Lifestyle team. I was blown away in another review, for Senior Director Samantha Perriello, by how often she communicates with lifestyle reporters on social media, specifically Instagram. When I think of TV news producers, and how I keep up with them and their roles and what they're covering, Instagram is not the social media platform that comes to mind. Most news producers and reporters live on Twitter—so that's where those on my broadcast team tend to keep up with reporters on social. Samantha, who has nearly 20 years of experience in PR, was sharing stories of how from her first few years working in PR in NYC and LA in her 20s, she made relationships with up-and-coming young reporters... and those relationships have lasted decades later. We were talking about the importance of meeting reporters in person and how not only is it fun to get together with the media, but it *always* pays off—and a lot of times, not in the way you necessarily think. I can't tell you how many times I've met up with a reporter and had an idea of a specific client I wanted to talk to them about... but the conversation naturally veered towards me sharing information about a different client.

By forming and then maintaining *genuine relationships* with the media, you will absolutely increase your likelihood of securing more media coverage for your clients. But not only will you increase the quantity of placements, you will also increase the power of each hit. Let me explain. Especially in the lifestyle space, those reporters have their own individual following. Samantha was sharing a story with me in her review about how she posted an Instagram story about a press hit she secured for a client in which she tagged the reporter, with whom she's friendly. That reporter then re-shared it to her network of *70,000* followers—this is an incredible number that adds to the impressions of the press placement.

Another example of the importance of forming genuine relationships with the media is that it can absolutely lead to new business! There have honestly been more times than I can count of an individual who is *not* repped by a PR firm, who's reached out to a producer or reporter about getting booked, and they have referred them to me. It's because I have build trust with those individuals and they know my reputation to be solid. Because of that I am someone who comes to mind when a situation like that arises. I'm grateful to all of those producers, but I also know it's because of my own hard work and dedication that those new business leads come in.

Business development is a core tenet of a thriving PR firm. Failure to secure new business is the number one reason most PR agencies—and businesses—fail. Securing new business is, similarly, not an exact science, but a commitment to reputation will definitely help to make the process easier. New business can come from *anywhere*—a family member, a former colleague, a neighbor, a media contact, you name it. It's a commitment to excellence that is at the cornerstone of any good referral.

One's ability to bring in new business will absolutely be an asset to anyone working at an agency. Most professionals working in the PR space do not have experience in bringing in clients. Unfortunately, even when many set their mind to it, and prioritize new business outreach, it still falls short. The primary reason for this lack of success is that, simply, bringing in new business is really difficult. Typically, the majority of new business at any agency falls on the shoulders of the founder and C-suite to prioritize, and most of the time they are successful simply because of their number of years working in the industry—the longer you work in an industry, hopefully, the more people you know and the stronger your reputation is, thus increasing the likelihood of a referral.

As mentioned, there's no real exact science to securing new business but there are a few tactics that will likely help to increase your chances of success. First, you have to get comfortable with promoting yourself and your achievements. It's an interesting quandary, but in my experience some of the best publicists I know are not the best at promoting themselves, either internally or to the world. Perhaps we chose this industry because we wanted to stay behind the scenes and lift others up. But if your goal is to secure new business, you have to let the world know how great you are at your job so that they can think of you for any referrals that they may have!

What I mean by "letting the world know how great you are" is to take various steps in your own promotion. The first, and probably the easiest, is to utilize your own social media to talk about your successes. Simple posts about recent press placements you secured for your clients can help in this regard. If you have developed an industry specialty, you can share how that area of your practice is growing and perhaps ask to connect with others in the space. When or if you achieve milestones, such as anniversaries at your place of employment, or win awards, or speak in public—all of these are opportunities to share with the world your achievements in PR. If your network doesn't know what you do—and furthermore isn't reminded frequently of what you do—your chances of having referrals come to you will be slimmer.

Referrals aren't the only lead for new business, but, in my 13 years of PR experience they are absolutely the best. Think about it—you have a client, or former client, who was so thrilled with the work you're doing that they took the time to connect you with another client who may want to hire you. It's the sincerest form of flattery and music to the ears of any agency owner. Once you get more established, you may want to consider strategically *asking* certain clients for introductions. This won't work with every client and this is where your own emotional intelligence will come into play. But for those current or former clients with whom you have a great relationship, it could work. I would recommend being strategic about the request; narrow down your options instead of asking for a blanket request of any introductions they could think of. Spend some time understanding who they are connected to; who their partners are; what types of professionals they work with frequently; maybe even go through their connections on LinkedIn so that you can ask for introductions with specificity.

It helps to create a capabilities deck so that when these types of opportunities arise, you will have something to immediately email over that could help to secure the business. A capabilities deck, or cap deck for short, typically is a PowerPoint or PDF that includes: a brief summary of the agency; one or two slides on the specifics of your area of expertise; three to five case study slides of current or former clients; the bios of those who work at the agency; and then pricing and contractual information.

The most important element of a cap deck is those case studies. At Pace, we select case studies where the industries match up with the prospective clients as a starting point, meaning, if we're courting a cyber security firm, we will highlight work we've done with other cyber clients in the past. The slide should be arranged wherein you include the client's name, a one- or two-sentence description of the focus of the work done together, and then clippings of the most impressive press placements you've secured for those clients—along with the total impressions those placements yielded. A cap deck is your opportunity to share your best work, so remember to put your best foot forward.

Also important to securing new business is networking. So many people hate the concept of networking. They think of it as painfully making small talk and normally can't wait to leave whatever networking event it is. But if you start to think of networking as an opportunity to simply meet people—it doesn't have to be transactional—then you may be able to have more fun in it. If you're going to work in PR, and in particular work at an agency, it really helps if you actually enjoy meeting and talking with people! The ability to connect and develop genuine relationships is key. By doing so and pushing yourself to go out and meet new people, not only will you be developing that important skill to do your job well, but you will undoubtedly start making connections that can lead to new business opportunities.

Another tactic is to invest in search engine optimization (SEO). SEO specialists help to optimize various links in a specialized way so that when others are searching in Google, it is more likely that your links will show up at the top of the search page. For example, if you type into Google "NYC PR firms," you'll see that my agency shows up on the first page of that search. This is incredible when you think about the fact that New York City is the hub for most media organizations and there are many, many others that are much larger, and have been in business longer than Pace PR has. But this is the power of SEO—it truly can give you a competitive edge.

In my experience, SEO really works best when you are creating new content that sends the message you want to promote in the world. I'll give you a real example. At my practice, we represent numerous attorneys and law firms. To attract new legal clients, I authored a piece titled "5 tips for becoming a legal pundit on TV" and shared it as a blog post on our company website. Here's what the article covered:

> Attorneys are not typically described as "shy," but taking a stance in the media can feel daunting. If you've ever wondered how to get on TV or in the public eye, there are several steps you can take to ensure you and your law firm stand out.
>
> Here are five tips for increasing your visibility in the media:
>
> 1 Create a media-friendly website with videos of past interviews or news clips, and a designated "media" tab to showcase your talking points.
>
> 2 Start a blog and position yourself as an expert by sharing your point of view on trials that are already in the media.

3 Utilize social media to share your blog posts and connect with journalists who cover legal news or trials in your area of expertise.

4 Determine which media outlets would best suit your practice and identify the appropriate reporters to connect with.

5 Avoid bombarding journalists at first; instead, position yourself as a valuable resource who can provide legal expertise in the context of larger trends or current events.

While these tips require significant time and effort, working with a PR agency that specializes in representing lawyers in the media can make the process easier.

As you can hopefully deduce, the headline was written in a manner that was intended to attract lawyers—that's what gets them to click on the link and read the article (also known as click-bait). But the last paragraph is what helps to sell Pace PR as an agency to hire. What I wrote is the truth—PR takes a *ton* of time. To secure earned media coverage is a labor of love—but when you *do* get a placement, if you truly love your job, it's a great feeling of accomplishment. I've seen it time and time again when professionals (not publicists) think they can do their own PR. And they might be able to for a short period of time. But, as I hope you've figured out by reading this book, it needs to be an ongoing process for it to be truly successful. And presumably, other professionals are busy in their own career, and don't have the time to continually keep up with producers and reporters, stay on top of the news and work on it day in and day out.

While I've laid out as many tactics as I can for successfully securing earned media coverage, there's one aspect that will undoubtedly play a role in your career: passion. No matter what career path you choose, if you don't have a passion for it, you may find success but you'll likely never reach your full potential. The same is doubly true for those who pursue a career in public relations. Why? Because it never stops. Many of us feel we're only as good as our last hit. But passion is needed to deal with the harsh rejection—or radio silence— that's often met when pitching the media. It's passion that keeps us all going, passion that drives us each and every day to do our best work for our clients. It's passion that motivates me to wake up at 6 am and start working; passion that has me following and keeping up with media on my social feeds; passion that has me reading and watching the news throughout the day; passion that motivates me to go above and beyond for my clients.

Public relations has become more important in today's modern business landscape. It is the art of building and maintaining relationships with the public and communicating messages that promote a brand's reputation and identity. However, to truly excel in the field of PR, it is essential to master the art of setting clear goals, crafting a well-crafted elevator pitch, establishing oneself as a thought leader, and more.

In the world of public relations, the importance of setting clear goals cannot be overstated. Without a sense of direction, all our efforts are for naught. Therefore, setting clear goals is crucial to the success of any PR campaign. A PR professional must clearly understand the objectives of their role in publicizing their brand or company. If these objectives are not clearly outlined, then it is time to take charge of their career and establish these goals for themselves. By doing so, they can develop targeted strategies that align with their overall objectives, driving results, and ultimately helping them achieve their desired outcomes.

Without a sense of direction, all our efforts are for naught. I encourage you to take stock of your happiness throughout this journey. Working in public relations and communications can be extremely challenging, but also very rewarding. If you realize that you don't have a true passion for storytelling for your clients, it's OK to consider another industry. We must know where we will make the most of the journey. However, if you can find your passion within PR, earned media coverage will undoubtedly follow, because where's there's passion, there's often success.

As you and I close this book, I invite you to embrace the insights and knowledge contained within its pages, whether you're a seasoned PR pro or a newcomer to the field. May it serve as a compass to guide you on the path to building successful brands through the power of public relations. I'm wishing you the best of luck and subsequent success on your PR and earned media journey, and hope I have made a small impact on your career through writing this book.

ACKNOWLEDGMENTS

In the words of Snoop Dogg, "I wanna thank me." Just kidding! But... seriously. As a business owner, professor, mother, wife, and daughter... writing a book at the same time was extremely challenging. I underestimated—greatly underestimated—how difficult it would be to write a book while also maintaining every other aspect of my life. Who I really want to acknowledge, first and foremost, are all of my fellow working mothers out there—especially those at Pace Public Relations. We all complete just about one million tasks per day, many of them unseen or unnoticed by others, to make our jobs, our homes, our lives run more smoothly. Well, I see you and I'd like to acknowledge you and the support I get from all my fellow working moms—you understand the struggle and without your support and friendship, all of this hard work would seem pointless.

My husband, Michael Sorrentino, continues to be my rock and without his encouragement I probably would have given up along this journey. Mike, watching you write and complete your book has absolutely motivated me to do the same. What I really want to acknowledge is your enthusiasm about this project. You reminded me to have fun along the way and to not take it too seriously. Your support at home also gave me the time I needed to actually write this book. I appreciate you so much. I love you—thank you.

Rose, one day when you're old enough to read this—thank you my little love for making me a mommy. As someone who is super type A and extremely career-driven, I definitely was a little nervous about how motherhood would impact my career. In fact, I was pretty sure becoming a mom would hurt my career. Boy, how it did just the opposite. Your arrival into this world crystallized to me what is actually important. You are the reason I began entrusting others at PPR in leadership roles—because I wanted to spend more time with you and focus on what truly mattered in my day to day. Becoming a mother actually showed me how much more I was capable of—it unleashed my inner superhero. Thank you for making me laugh every single day and for snuggling me on the couch as I wrote this book.

Thank you to my team at Pace PR – this book definitely took up a lot of my time and focus and you all stepped up and made sure the wheels kept moving. I appreciate you all endlessly.

Jordi Lippe-McGraw… thank you for helping me in the final days to edit this manuscript into its final condition. I really couldn't have done it without you.

My editor, Bronwyn Geyer, played a seminal role in this process, both in keeping me on track and providing all the right kinds of encouragement. Thank you.

And finally, this book wouldn't have been possible without the woman who gave me life, my mother, Susan Pace Scranton. There's no love like a mother's love and your implicit encouragement and belief in me is everything. I love you to the moon and back.

NOTES

1 PR and Successful Branding

1 PRSA. About, Public Relations Society of America, nd. www.prsa.org/about (archived at https://perma.cc/YCC7-NFF8)

2 Oxford Learner's Dictionaries. Marketing, Oxford Learner's Dictionaries, nd. www.oxfordlearnersdictionaries.com/us/definition/english/marketing (archived at https://perma.cc/S4QH-J2FV)

3 Oxford Reference. Public relations, Oxford Reference, nd. www.oxfordreference.com/view/10.1093/oi/authority.20110803100353641 (archived at https://perma.cc/QT3U-VFVC)

4 C Aragão. Gender pay gap in U.S. hasn't changed much in two decades, Pew Research Center, March 1, 2023. www.pewresearch.org/fact-tank/2023/03/01/gender-pay-gap-facts (archived at https://perma.cc/3TLF-9C48)

5 Glassdoor Team. 50 HR & recruiting stats that make you think, Glassdoor, December 21, 2018. www.glassdoor.com/employers/blog/50-hr-recruiting-stats-make-think (archived at https://perma.cc/SQ28-LBVB)

6 R. Thomas et al. (2022) *Women in the Workplace 2022*, McKinsey & Company and Lean In. https://wiw-report.s3.amazonaws.com/Women_in_the_Workplace_2022.pdf (archived at https://perma.cc/47BF-J8PJ)

7 Oxford Reference. Mission statement, Oxford Reference, nd. www.oxfordreference.com/display/10.1093/oi/authority.20110826110258868 (archived at https://perma.cc/ZUM8-CJK5)

2 The Three Spheres of Influence in Media

1 Pew Research Center. Newspapers fact sheet. Pew Research Center's Journalism Project, Pew Research Center, June 29, 2021. www.pewresearch.org/journalism/fact-sheet/newspapers (archived at https://perma.cc/7TG7-4A44)

2 A. Grundy. Service annual survey shows continuing decline in print publishing revenue, United States Census Bureau, June 7, 2022.

www.census.gov/library/stories/2022/06/internet-crushes-traditional-media.html (archived at https://perma.cc/B5FQ-X9XQ)

3 E. Varagouli. How to measure SEO performance and results, Semrush, October 29, 2020. www.semrush.com/blog/seo-results (archived at https://perma.cc/W4E6-GCFD)

4 P. Syme. FTX spent nearly $7 million on food and over $15 million on luxury Bahamian hotels in just 9 months, court documents show, Business Insider, January 6, 2023. www.businessinsider.com/ftx-spent-7-million-on-meals-entertainment-luxury-hotels-bahamas-2023-1 (archived at https://perma.cc/NC6L-T7G7)

5 J. Kelly. CEO who fired 900 employees via a Zoom video and called his employees "dumb dolphins" had a mass layoff—some workers found out by seeing their bank account, Forbes, October 12, 2022. www.forbes.com/sites/jackkelly/2022/03/09/ceo-who-fired-900-employees-via-a-zoom-video-and-called-his-employees-dumb-dolphins-had-a-mass-layoff-some-workers-found-out-by-seeing-their-bank-account (archived at https://perma.cc/6ABY-2BK3)

6 E. R. Connolly. TV advertising costs: What you can expect to pay locally and nationally, Fast Capital 360, December 28, 2021. www.fastcapital360.com/blog/how-much-do-tv-commercials-cost (archived at https://perma.cc/MAC7-LGLW)

3 Origin Story

1 Oliver. The origin stories behind 5 famous brands, Looka, August 15, 2019. https://looka.com/blog/famous-brands-origin-stories (archived at https://perma.cc/WH77-KWRJ)

6 Thought Leadership

1 S. Schooley. What is thought leadership, and why does it matter? Business News Daily, February 24, 2023. www.businessnewsdaily.com/9253-thought-leadership.html (archived at https://perma.cc/C6QA-RMQV)

2 While creating your own podcast and videos are certainly a part of owned media, the strategy there is slightly different, which is why I'm not including them in this bucket.

INDEX